MACARON R

FOR BEGINNERS

MACARON HEAVEN!

60 Macaron Recipes

To Delight Everyone

ASHLYN SCOTT

Copyright © 2020 Ashlyn Scott

All Rights Reserved

Copyright 2020 By Ashlyn Scott - All rights reserved.

The following book is produced below with the goal of providing information that is as accurate and reliable as possible. Regardless, purchasing this eBook can be seen as consent to the fact that both the publisher and the author of this book are in no way experts on the topics discussed within and that any recommendations or suggestions that are made herein are for entertainment purposes only. Professionals should be consulted as needed prior to undertaking any of the action endorsed herein.

This declaration is deemed fair and valid by both the American Bar Association and the Committee of Publishers Association and is legally binding throughout the United States.

Furthermore, the transmission, duplication or reproduction of any of the following work including specific information will be considered an illegal act irrespective of if it is done electronically or in print. This extends to creating a secondary or tertiary copy of the work or a recorded copy and is only allowed with express written consent from the Publisher. All additional right reserved.

The information in the following pages is broadly considered to be a truthful and accurate account of facts and as such any inattention, use or misuse of the information in question by the reader will render any resulting actions solely under their purview. There are no scenarios in which the publisher or the original author of this work can be in any fashion deemed liable for any hardship or damages that may befall them after undertaking information described herein.

Additionally, the information in the following pages is intended only for informational purposes and should thus be thought of as universal. As befitting its nature, it is presented without assurance regarding its prolonged validity or interim quality. Trademarks that are mentioned are done without written consent and can in no way be considered an endorsement from the trademark holder.

Table of Contents

PART I 11

    Classic Vanilla Macaron 12

Chapter 1: Fruity Macaron Recipes 15

    Strawberry Rosé Macarons 15

    Rosé Buttercream 17

    Strawberry Macarons 17

    Blueberry Filled Macarons 18

    Orange Macarons 19

    19

    Lemon Macarons 21

    Mango Macarons 22

    Mango Buttercream 23

    Coconut-Lavender Macarons 23

    Lavender Buttercream 24

    Passionfruit Macarons 25

    Bananas Foster Macarons 27

Chapter 2: Chocolate Macarons 29

    Classic Chocolate Macarons 29

    Classic Chocolate Ganache 30

    Cookies n' Cream Macarons 31

    Chocolate Caramel Coconut Macarons 32

    Mint Chocolate Macarons 33

    Chocolate Covered Strawberry Macarons 34

    Chocolate Macarons With Salted Caramel Filling 35

Chocolate Peanut Butter Macarons 36

Chocolate Raspberry Macarons 37

Chocolate Macarons With Caramelized White Chocolate Filling 38

Chocolate Cream Filling 39

Chapter 3: Nutty Macarons 40

Classic Peanut Macarons 40

Pistachio and Chocolate Macarons 42

PB&J Macarons 43

Peanut Butter and Honey Macarons 44

Chocolate Nutella Macarons 45

Pecan Pie Macarons 46

Maple Walnut Macarons 47

White Chocolate Macadamia Nut Macarons 50

Chapter 4: Coffee, Matcha, and Other Drink Macarons 51

Classic Coffee Macarons 51

Classic Coffee Filling 52

Classic Matcha Macarons 53

Vanilla Macchiato Macarons 54

Coffee Caramel Macarons 55

Espresso Mocha Macarons 56

Hazelnut Coffee Macarons 58

Matcha Mango Macarons 59

Matcha Raspberry Macarons 60

Thai Tea Macarons 61

Pumpkin Spice Latte Macarons 62

Spiced Chai Macarons 64

Create Classic Vanilla Buttercream recipe, then fill cooled macarons,

taking the cookies and piping along the flat side, then sandwiching it together with a second cookie. Let set in fridge overnight 65

PART II 66

Smoothie Diet Recipes 67

    Chapter 1: Fruit Smoothies 68

        Quick Fruit Smoothie 68

        Triple Threat Smoothie 70

        Tropical Smoothie 71

        Fruit and Mint Smoothie 72

        Banana Smoothie 74

        Dragon Fruit Smoothie 76

        Kefir Blueberry Smoothie 78

        Ginger Fruit Smoothie 80

        Fruit Batido 82

        Banana Peanut Butter Smoothie 83

    Chapter 2: Breakfast Smoothies 84

        Berry Banana Smoothie 84

        Berry Surprise 85

        Coconut Matcha Smoothie 87

        Cantaloupe Frenzy 88

        Berry Lemon Smoothie 89

        Orange Glorious 91

        Grapefruit Smoothie 92

        Sour Smoothie 93

        Ginger Orange Smoothie 94

        Cranberry Smoothie 95

        Creamsicle Smoothie 97

Sunshine Smoothie 98

Chapter 3: Vegetable Smoothies 99

Mango Kale Berry Smoothie 99

Breakfast Pink Smoothie..100

Butternut Squash Smoothie 102

Zucchini and Wild Blueberry Smoothie 103

Cauliflower and Blueberry Smoothie 104

Immunity Booster Smoothie 105

Ginger, Carrot, and Turmeric Smoothie 108

Romaine Mango Smoothie 110

Fig Zucchini Smoothie...111

Carrot Peach Smoothie 112

Sweet Potato and Mango Smoothie 114

Carrot Cake Smoothie..115

Chapter 4: Green Smoothies..116

Kale Avocado Smoothie 116

Celery Pineapple Smoothie..118

Cucumber Mango and Lime Smoothie 119

Kale, Melon, and Broccoli Smoothie 121

Kiwi Spinach Smoothie 123

Avocado Smoothie 124

PART III...125

Chapter 1: The Fundamentals of a Low Sugar Diet for Diabetics 126

Chapter 2: Benefits of a Low Sugar Diet for Diabetics 129

Chapter 3: Savory Recipe Ideas 132

Savory Idea #1: Tangy Cabbage Treat....................................132

Savory Idea #2: Low-carb Egg &Veggie Bites 134

Savory Idea #3: Yummy Chicken Dee-light 136

Savory Idea #4: Low-carb Fried Chicken Surprise 138

Savory Idea #5: Low-Sugar Beef Explosion 140

Savory Idea #6: Tangy Pork Extravaganza 142

Savory Idea #7: Filet & Cheese Supreme 144

Savory Idea #8: Quick and Easy Low-carb Chips 145

Savory Idea #9: Unbelievably Low-carb South Treat 146

Savory Idea #10: Low-sugar Italian Snack Option 148

Chapter 4: Gourmet Recipe Ideas 150

Gourmet Idea #1: Tasty Chicken and Veggie Pot 150

Gourmet Idea #2: Delicious Low-sugar Chicken Meal 151

Gourmet Idea #3: Italian Chicken Dinner Delight 153

Gourmet Idea #4: Yummy Lemon Beef Surprise 155

Gourmet Idea #5: Gourmet Sirloin Option 157

Gourmet Idea #6: Unbelievably Low-sugar Surprise 159

Gourmet Idea #7: Low-carb Salmon Delight 160

Gourmet Idea #8: Shrimp-Avocado Treat 162

Gourmet Idea #9: Gourmet Hot Pot Surprise 163

Gourmet Idea #10: Low-carb Tuna Wraps Treat 164

Chapter 5: Quick and Easy Recipe Ideas 165

Quick and Easy Idea #1: Quick and Easy Veggie Treat 165

Quick and Easy Idea #2: Spicy Egg and Veggie Dash 167

Quick and Easy Idea #3: Low-sugar Hot Cake Surprise 168

Quick and Easy Idea #4: Cheesy Veggie Bites 170

Quick and Easy Idea #5: Low-carb Pudding Dee-light 172

Quick and Easy Idea #6: Tangy Egg Salad 173

Quick and Easy Idea #7: Cheesy Egg Cups 175

Quick and Easy Idea #8: Asparagus Appetizer/Side Salad 177

Quick and Easy Idea #9: Low-carb Pork Treat 178

Quick and Easy Idea #10: Easy Fish Delight 180

Chapter 6: Low-Carb Recipe Ideas 181

Low-Carb Recipe Idea #1: Balsamic Roast Delight 181

Low-Carb Recipe Idea #2: Burger Calzone Treat 183

Low-Carb Recipe Idea #3: Steak Skillet Nacho 185

Low-Carb Recipe Idea #4: Portobello Burger Meal 187

Low-Carb Recipe Idea #5: Low-carb Super Chili 189

Low-Carb Recipe Idea #6: "You won't believe it's low-carb" Chicken Parmesan 190

Low-Carb Recipe Idea #7: Tangy Coconut Chicken 192

Low-Carb Recipe Idea #8: Slow cook Chicken Casserole 195

Low-Carb Recipe Idea #9: Low-carb Roll Up Treat 196

Low-Carb Recipe Idea #10: Cauliflower Cheese Surprise 198

Chapter 7: 7-day Sample Low Sugar Diet Plan 199

PART I

Classic Vanilla Macaron

This recipe will provide you with the foundation for many of the recipes that will be listed in the future chapters. This, paired with the classic buttercream, will create the traditionally flavored cookies that can be changed into a wide variety of flavors.

Ingredients

- Almond flour (1 c.)
- Egg whites (3, room temperature)
- Food coloring gel (2-3 drops of color of choice—make sure it is gel, not liquid)
- Granulated sugar (0.25 c.)
- Powdered sugar (1.75 c.)
- Salt (1 tsp)

- Vanilla extract (0.5 tsp.)

Instructions

1. Take your flour, powdered sugar, and half of your salt and run them through a food processor to create an extra fine powder. Then, take a sieve to pour it into a bowl.
2. Separately, beat egg whites and remaining salt until it begins to form peaks. Slowly add granulated sugar until it is completely combined but not overmixed. It will form stiff peaks that will not fall when turned upside down.
3. Mix in vanilla and food coloring until just mixed.
4. With around a third of your almond flour mix at a time, combine it into the egg whites with a spatula to fold gently. It is combined well when batter falls off of spatula in ribbons.
5. Move batter to a piping bag with a rounded tip. Secure parchment paper in place with dots of batter in the corners on the baking sheet.
6. Make macarons with 1.5-inch circles onto the parchment paper, roughly 1 inch apart. Gently tap the baking sheet on your counter five times to allow air bubbles to escape.
7. Leave macarons sitting at room temperature for an hour. They should be dry on the surface.
8. Warm oven to 300F, and when heated, bake for 17 minutes. Macarons should no longer stick to the paper.
9. Leave macarons on a wire rack to cool before filling.
10. To fill, take buttercream and put a dollop on one shell and then place the second one on top to create a sandwich. Allow them to sit for 24 hours and serve.

Classic Vanilla Buttercream Filling

This will provide you with the classic vanilla buttercream filling that goes into macarons. This is a base for all sorts of other flavors as well. You will see this recipe referenced a lot throughout the future chapters, and this flavor for buttercream will go with just about any cookie that you will see.

Ingredients

- Butter (1 c. unsalted, room temp)
- Heavy cream (3 Tbsp.)
- Powdered sugar (3 c.)
- Vanilla extract (1 tsp)

Instructions

1. Beat the butter until it has become fluffy, typically around a minute. Then, using a sieve, slowly incorporate your powdered sugar until it is entirely combined. Then, combine in the vanilla, beating it. 1 Tbsp. at a time, add in your cream until it has become the right texture. Then, transfer to a piping bag.

Chapter 1: Fruity Macaron Recipes

Strawberry Rosé Macarons

Ingredients

- Classic Macaron Recipe (without vanilla)

- Rosé reduction
- Rosé buttercream (see next recipe)

Rosé reduction:

- Sparkling rosé (1 c.)
- Strawberries (1 c., sliced)

Instructions

1. Prepare your rosé reduction by simmering the rosé and strawberries on a moderately high temperature for between 6 and 8 minutes until it has reduced down to just 0.25 c. of liquid. Strain the liquid and allow it to cool.
2. Prepare Classic Macaron Recipe to Step 3 and substitute in 2 tsp of rosé reduction for vanilla, then continue the recipe as is.
3. Pair with rosé buttercream.

Rosé Buttercream

Ingredients

- Dehydrated strawberries (0.33 c.)
- Powdered sugar (1 c.)
- Salt (just a pinch)
- Unsalted butter (0.5 stick, softened)
- Rosé reduction (2 Tbsp.—see previous recipe)

Instructions

1. Powder your dehydrated strawberries in a food processor.
2. Beat butter until fluffy, about a minute, then mix in half of your sugar, salt, and your powdered strawberries. Mix well, then sift remaining sugar and beat. Combine in 2 Tbsp. rose reduction and combine until fluffy.
3. Transfer to a piping bag.

Strawberry Macarons

Ingredients

- Classic Macaron Recipe (leave out vanilla)
- Strawberry emulsion (1 tsp)
- Classic Vanilla Buttercream recipe

Instructions

1. Prepare Classic Vanilla Macaron recipe to step 3. Omit vanilla and substitute in 1 tsp of strawberry emulsion instead. Continue through recipe.
2. Finish with Classic Vanilla Buttercream recipe.

Blueberry Filled Macarons

Ingredients

- Classic Vanilla Macarons Recipe (Use blue or turquoise coloring gel)
- Classic Vanilla Buttercream Recipe
- Blueberry Filling

For blueberry filling:

- Blueberries (7 oz., fresh or frozen)
- White sugar (0.25 c.)
- Cornstarch (1 Tbsp.)
- Lemon juice (1 Tbsp.)
- Water (0.5 c.)

Instructions

1. Prepare macarons according to recipe.
2. Prepare buttercream according to recipe.
3. Start blueberry filling. Begin with berries mixed in a small pot with the lemon, sugar, and half of the water. Cook on a moderately low temperature until all sugar has dissolved away.
4. Separately, mix cornstarch with the last 0.25 c. of water. Then, combine the starch mixture into the blueberries on low heat. Continue to cook until it becomes thick and glossy. Mixture is done when it coats a spoon. Let cool before you use it.
5. To prepare macarons, place filling, and frosting in piping bags. Create a ring with the buttercream around the perimeter of the cookie, and then put in a dollop of the blueberry filling within the middle. Place another cookie on top to seal. Keep refrigerated.

Orange Macarons

Ingredients

- Classic Macaron Recipe (omit vanilla—add in 0.5 tsp each orange zest and orange extract instead, and use orange food coloring)
- Classic Vanilla Buttercream recipe
- Orange curd filling

For orange curd filling:

- Butter (0.5 c., unsalted and chilled, cut into cubes)

- Cornstarch (2 Tbsp.)
- Egg (1 whole large)
- Egg yolks (3 from large eggs)
- Lemon juice (4 Tbsp.)
- Lemon zest (0.5 Tbsp.)
- Orange juice (0.75 c.)
- Orange zest (0.5 Tbsp.)
- Salt (0.25 tsp)
- Sugar (0.5 c.)

Instructions

1. Follow the recipe for Classic Vanilla Macarons to step 3—then omit vanilla and substitute in the zest and extract. Continue recipe as listed.
2. Prepare buttercream recipe.
3. Create an orange curd filling. Warm orange juice for 30 seconds in microwave.
4. Prepare a double boiler. In the top bowl, before it is on the heat, mix together egg, yolks, zests, sugar, salt, and starch. Mix it together until it is fluffy. Then slowly incorporate the juices. Place concoction onto double boiler and cook on low. After about 10 minutes, the foam from whipping should begin to disappear as the entire thing thickens. It is done when the mixture will coat a spatula.
5. Take it off of the heat and add single cubes of butter, one at a time, melting each one down before adding the next. Continue to mix, then let cool. It should be thick.
6. Strain through a sieve to remove zest and place in a piping bag when cool.
7. To assemble cookies, take one macaron and pipe a ring of vanilla buttercream around the outside. Then, fill with orange curd. Top with second cookie and let set. Store in fridge.

Lemon Macarons

Ingredients

- Classic Vanilla Macaron Recipe (omit vanilla and substitute in 0.5 tsp each lemon zest and lemon extract instead)
- Classic Vanilla Buttercream Recipe
- Lemon Curd

For the lemon curd:

- Egg yolks (3 large)
- Egg (1 whole, large)
- Cornstarch (2 Tbsp.)
- Salt (0.5 tsp)
- Lemon zest (1 Tbsp.)
- Lemon juice (0.75 c.)
- Sugar (0.75 c.)
- Butter (0.5 c., cold, unsalted, and cut into cubes)

Instructions

1. Prepare Classic Vanilla Macaron Recipe to step 3, then substitute 0.5 tsp lemon zest and 0.5 tsp lemon extract for vanilla. Use yellow food coloring. Then, continue recipe as directed.
2. Prepare Classic Vanilla Buttercream recipe as directed.
3. Start the lemon curd. Warm lemon juice for 30 seconds in microwave.
4. Prepare a double boiler. In the top bowl, before it is on the heat, mix together egg, yolks, zest, sugar, salt, and starch. Mix it together until it is fluffy. Then slowly incorporate the juices. Place concoction onto double boiler and cook on low. After about 10 minutes, the foam from whipping should begin to disappear as the entire thing thickens. It is done when the mixture will coat a spatula.
5. Take it off of the heat and add single cubes of butter, one at a time, melting each one down before adding the next. Continue to mix, then let cool. It should be thick.
6. Strain through a sieve to remove zest and place in a piping bag when cool.
7. To assemble cookies, take one macaron and pipe a ring of vanilla buttercream around the outside. Then, fill with lemon curd. Top with second cookie and let set. Store in fridge.

Mango Macarons
Ingredients

- Classic Vanilla Macaron Recipe
- Mango Buttercream (see next recipe)

Instructions

1. Follow the recipe for classic vanilla macarons (orange food coloring)
2. Use mango buttercream to fill them.

Mango Buttercream

Pairs well with classic macarons, or try adding it to other flavors as well

Ingredients

- Butter (0.25 c., salted)
- Fresh mango juice (3 Tbsp.—you can extract this with a sieve and slices of half a mango)
- Powdered sugar (0.75 c.)

Instructions

1. Beat butter until fluffy and pale. Then, slowly incorporate your sugar. Continue to mix and beat until you have the texture of buttercream.
2. Extract mango juice and mix it into the buttercream. Transfer buttercream into a piping bag and use.

Coconut-Lavender Macarons

Ingredients

- Classic Macaron Recipe (omit vanilla extract and substitute with 0.5 tsp coconut extract instead)
- Lavender Buttercream (see next recipe)

Instructions

1. Prepare classic macarons until step 3, then substitute coconut extract for vanilla. Continue as directed and assemble with lavender buttercream.

Lavender Buttercream

Ingredients

- Lavender flowers (1 Tbsp., dried)
- Powdered sugar (1.5 c.)
- Unsalted butter (4 Tbsp., room temperature)
- Vanilla extract (0.5 tsp)
- Violet or lavender food coloring (10-15 drops)
- Whole milk (0.25 c.)

Instructions

1. Mix together your milk and lavender flowers into a small pot. Warm it until the edges begin to bubble a bit, but do not let it get to a simmer. Remove from heat and let cool to room temperature. Then, strain out the flowers from milk.
2. Beat butter together with vanilla until creamy and fluffy. Then, mix in the sugar, milk, and food coloring. Beat until fluffy and the texture of frosting. Put into a piping bag and use.

Passionfruit Macarons
Ingredients

- Classic Vanilla Macarons recipe (omitting vanilla and using yellow food coloring)
- Passionfruit curd
- Tempered marshmallow frosting

For the passionfruit curd:

- Butter (3 Tbsp., unsalted)
- Egg yolks (2)
- Granulated sugar (3 Tbsp.)
- Passion fruit pulp (0.25 c.)
- Sea salt (0.25 tsp)

For the marshmallow frosting

- Cream of tartar (0.25 tsp)
- Egg whites (2)
- Granulated sugar (0.5 c.)
- Sea salt (0.125 tsp)
- Vanilla extract (1 tsp)

Instructions

1. Prepare the macarons according to the recipe, omitting the vanilla entirely.
2. Create your marshmallow frosting. Set up a double boiler over medium heat. Combine all ingredients but vanilla into a bowl, then set the bowl over the water. Whisk until the mixture reaches 140F. Then, move the

mixture to your stand mixer and whip for 5 minutes until it begins to create a thicker frosting. Add in the vanilla and combine well. Put mixture into a piping bag.
3. Prepare your passionfruit curd. Cream the butter for roughly 30 seconds, then mix in the salt and sugar for another minute. Mix in egg yolk, one at a time, until well mixed. Add in the passionfruit pulp and mix well. It might seem separated—this is fine at this step.
4. Move to a saucepan and cook at low heat while constantly stirring. You want to keep it below a boil and do not stop mixing. When the curd can coat a spoon, it is done.
5. Assemble by taking cookie, then piping a circle with the marshmallow frosting around the outside. Fill with passionfruit curd. Keep refrigerated.

Bananas Foster Macarons

Ingredients

- Classic Vanilla Macarons recipe (substitute out the vanilla for 1 tsp of banana extract instead, and use 4-5 drops of yellow food coloring gel)
- Bananas foster buttercream filling
- Caramel sauce (2 Tbsp.)

For the bananas foster buttercream filling:

- Banana (1, mashed)
- Banana extract (0.5 tsp)
- Butter (0.5 c., unsalted at room temperature)
- Powdered sugar (4 c.)
- Rum extract (0.25 tsp)

Instructions

1. Prepare macarons according to Classic Vanilla Macarons recipe, omitting the vanilla and substituting in 1 tsp of banana extract instead. Otherwise, follow all instructions accordingly.

2. While macarons bake, prepare your buttercream filling. To do so, cream your butter, then incorporate in the banana. Mix well, then start to cream in the powdered sugar.

3. Beat until sugar mixture is nice and smooth, then add together the extracts as well. Place cream mixture into a piping bag.

4. To assemble, put the mixture on the flat side of the macaron, creating a ring. Then, place in a small dollop (roughly 0.25 tsp) of caramel sauce into the centers of the filling. Sandwich together the macarons, then keep refrigerated in an airtight container.

Chapter 2: Chocolate Macarons

Classic Chocolate Macarons

Ingredients

- Almond flour (1.33 c.)
- Cocoa powder (0.25 c., unsweetened, plus extra to dust)
- Egg whites (4, room temperature)
- Powdered sugar (2 cups + 2 Tbsp.)

Instructions

1. Prepare baking sheets with parchment paper and set up a pastry bag with a large round tip.
2. Sift almond flour, powdered sugar, and cocoa into a bowl.
3. Beat egg whites until foamy. Then whip into peaks. Use a spatula to gently fold dry ingredients into the egg mixture. It should look like cake batter.
4. Place mixture into piping bag and pipe onto sheet in 1.5-inch rounds with 1 inch between.
5. Tap pan on the counter a few times to release air bubbles.
6. Set cookies aside to rest for 30 minutes-1 hour until crunchy on the top. Then, preheat oven to 425F.
7. When cookies go in, drop the temperature down to 350 F and keep the door cracked. Cook for 10 minutes until firm.
8. Put cookies onto a cooling rack, preheat to 425 again, and follow the same process for the second pan of cookies. Let cool completely before frosting.

Classic Chocolate Ganache

Ingredients

- Bittersweet chocolate (4 oz., chopped)
- Butter (2 Tbsp., unsalted, room temperature)
- Heavy cream (0.5 c.)

Instructions

1. Place chocolate in a mixing bowl.
2. Heat up your cream until beginning to bubble. Mix in the chocolate carefully without whipping any bubbles in. Wait for a minute, then mix in the butter until it is smooth.
3. Chill in fridge for about 30 minutes. It should be smooth and spreadable, but thick. Pour ganache into a piping bag to use.

Cookies n' Cream Macarons
Ingredients

- Egg whites (3, room temperature)
- Almond flour (0.75 c.)
- Dark cocoa powder (2 Tbsp.)
- Black food coloring gel (0.5 tsp)
- Sugar (0.25 c.)
- Crushed chocolate cookies (0.25 c. For best results use Oreos and reserve filling)
- Powdered sugar (1.25 c.)

For cookie cream Buttercream

- Butter (1 c., softened)
- Powdered sugar (2 c.)
- Vanilla (1 tsp)
- Milk (2 Tbsp.)
- Cookie filling (0.5 c., reserved from Oreos)

Instructions

1. Beat eggs until frothy, then incorporate the sugar until it becomes stiff peaks.
2. Put cookie crumbs, almond flour, cocoa powder, and powdered sugar into a sieve and slowly combine, folding gently to avoid overmixing.
3. Add food coloring until just combined
4. Preheat oven to 285 F and pipe cookies onto a baking sheet lined with parchment paper. Cookies should be roughly 1.5 inches and 1 inch apart. Give the pan a few quick taps on the counter to get out air bubbles.
5. Leave cookies to rest for an hour until dry to the touch. Bake for 15 minutes.
6. Prepare filling. Mix butter, sugar, cookie cream, vanilla, and milk until the consistency of frosting, then set aside in piping bag.
7. Let cool, then fill with buttercream. Keep refrigerated.

Chocolate Caramel Coconut Macarons
Ingredients

- Classic Chocolate Macaron Recipe
- Caramel coconut filling

For caramel coconut filling:

- Caramel chews (20, unwrapped)
- Milk (1 Tbsp.)
- Salt (pinch)
- Shredded coconut (0.75 c., sweetened)

Instructions

1. Prepare chocolate macarons according to Classic Chocolate Macaron recipe.
2. Prepare your filling. To create the filling, warm oven to 300F. Then, put coconut across a parchment-lined baking pan. Let it toast for between 10 and 20 minutes until golden, stirring every few minutes. Allow to cool.
3. Microwave caramels, milk, and a pinch of salt, stirring every 30 seconds until smooth, usually 1-2 minutes. Then, mix coconut into the caramel.
4. Coat two teaspoons in cooking spray and put filling onto macaron shells to sandwich together.

Mint Chocolate Macarons

Ingredients

- Classic Chocolate Macarons
- Mint Ganache

For the mint ganache:

- Chocolate chips (0.25 c.)
- Crème de menthe pieces (0.25 c.)
- Heavy cream (0.33 c.)

Instructions

1. Prepare the macarons according to directions in Classic Chocolate Macarons recipe.
2. To create the ganache, place cream, chocolate, and crème de menthe into a glass measuring cup. Microwave for half a minute, then combine well. If necessary to finish melting everything, microwave another 15 seconds. Whisk together until well incorporated, then chill until thickened.
3. Assemble cookies and then chill overnight in fridge.

Chocolate Covered Strawberry Macarons

Ingredients

- Classic Chocolate Macaron Recipe
- Strawberry buttercream

For strawberry buttercream:

- Butter (0.25 c., softened)
- Powdered sugar (2 c.)
- Strawberry extract (2 tsp)

Instructions

1. Prepare chocolate macarons according to Classic Chocolate Macaron recipe.
2. Make buttercream by placing butter, softened, into a bowl, and fluffing it with powdered sugar. Then, incorporate the strawberry extract. Assemble like usual.

Chocolate Macarons With Salted Caramel Filling

Ingredients

- Classic Chocolate Macaron Recipe
- Caramel filling

For the caramel filling:

- Butter (5 Tbsp. unsalted, cubed and cold)
- Cream (3 Tbsp. cream)
- Salt crystals (0.5 tsp)
- Sugar (0.5 c.)

Instructions

1. Prepare macarons according to the Classic Chocolate Macaron recipe.
2. Create filling. To do so, warm cream until it barely reaches a boil at moderate heat. Set cream aside. Then, put your sugar into a thick, heavy saucepan at medium-high heat and cook without disturbing it. Wait for the sugar to dissolve and become caramel colored. Then, remove and add in cream. Expect it to bubble, and mix in with a wooden spoon for about a minute.
3. Remove the mixture from heat and mix in salt and butter, cube by cube, stirring to incorporate it. Put it into a bowl and chill in the fridge.
4. Smear a layer of caramel onto one macaron and sandwich together to assemble.

Chocolate Peanut Butter Macarons

Ingredients

- Classic Chocolate Macaron Recipe
- Peanut Butter Filling

For peanut butter filling:

- Creamy peanut butter (0.5 c.)
- Powdered sugar (0.5 c.)
- Salt (0.125 tsp)
- Unsalted butter (2 Tbsp., room temperature)
- Vanilla extract (0.5 tsp)
- Milk to thin as needed

Instructions

1. Prepare macarons according to Classic Chocolate Macaron Recipe.
2. To make the filling, beat butter and peanut butter until well combined. Then, toss in the sugar, vanilla, and salt. Carefully bring up in speed and beat until light. If too thick, add a Tbsp. of milk to try to thin it out.
3. Place in a piping bag and fill cookies to serve. Keep refrigerated.

Chocolate Raspberry Macarons

Ingredients

- Classic Chocolate Macarons Recipe
- Raspberry Buttercream

Raspberry buttercream:

- Butter (2 Tbsp., unsalted at room temperature)
- Powdered sugar (1 c.)
- Raspberry jam (2 Tbsp.)

Instructions

1. Prepare Chocolate Macarons to recipe.
2. Assemble your raspberry buttercream. To do so, beat butter and jam together until they are well combined. Then, add in powdered sugar, mixing well until you get a fluffy frosting. Expect it to be firm, but still malleable.
3. Pipe or spread filling into cooled macarons.

Chocolate Macarons With Caramelized White Chocolate Filling

Ingredients

- Classic Chocolate Macaron recipe
- Caramelized white chocolate

Caramelized white chocolate:

- Flaky sea salt (pinch to taste)
- White chocolate (24 oz., at least 30% cocoa butter)

Instructions

1. Prepare macarons according to Classic Chocolate Macaron recipe.
2. Create your filling. To do so, warm the oven to 250F. Then, chop chocolate into small, coarse pieces. Place chocolate on rimmed baking sheet and bake it for the next 10 minutes. Pull it out and spread melted chocolate across the pan to create even layers. Cook for 30-60 more minutes, stirring every 10. It might look unpleasant, but keep stirring and mixing. It will caramelize.
3. Cook until it becomes golden brown. Then, toss a pinch of salt atop it and mix well. Spread between macarons.

Chocolate Cream Filling

Ingredients

- Bittersweet chocolate (4 oz., chopped)
- Butter (1 Tbsp.)
- Corn syrup (2 tsp)
- Heavy whipping cream (0.5 c.)

Instructions

1. Place chocolate into its own bowl. Then, take a saucepan and warm cream and syrup until barely boiling.
2. Pour the cream mixture over the chocolate and mix together until smooth.
3. Gently combine in butter until melted and incorporated.
4. Allow it to cool, stirring every now and then, until thick. Spread or pipe onto cookies.

Chapter 3: Nutty Macarons

Classic Peanut Macarons

Ingredients

- Powdered sugar (2.33 c.)
- Roasted peanuts (1.33 c., unsalted)

- Granulated sugar (0.33 c.)
- Egg whites (4)
- Classic Chocolate Ganache recipe

Instructions

1. Process your powdered sugar and peanuts until finely ground into a flour-like consistency.
2. Warm a pan over medium heat with maybe 3 inches of water. Let it boil, then reduce temperature to a low simmer. Take a large bowl and whisk your eggs and granulated sugar. Then, place the bowl over the water in the pan, creating a double boiler, and stir until sugar is dissolved and the mix feels warm. Take the bowl off of water and beat to stiff peaks.
3. Gently mix together your powdered sugar mix.
4. When mixed well, spoon batter into a pastry bag and make 1.5-inch rounds, 1 inch apart on a parchment-lined sheet. Tap pan on the counter to release air bubbles.
5. Let cookies rest for 30 minutes to dry, then bake for 15 minutes at 300F.
6. Allow cookies to cool on sheets, then remove gently.
7. Prepare Classic Chocolate Ganache recipe.
8. Fill cookies with chocolate ganache, then place a second cookie atop to make a sandwich.

Pistachio and Chocolate Macarons

Ingredients

- Egg whites (3)
- Pistachios (0.75 c.)
- Powdered sugar (1.25 c.)
- Salt (pinch)
- Sugar (0.25 c.)
- Chocolate Cream Filling Recipe

Instructions

1. Allow egg whites to come up to room temperature. While waiting, take powdered sugar and pistachios and process them until they become a fine powder, similar in texture to flour.
2. Warm oven to 350F. Add in a pinch of salt to your egg whites and then beat until they begin to make peaks. Gently add in 1 Tbsp. of sugar at a time until completely combined, beating until you get thick, stiff peaks.
3. Mix in your pistachio flour mixture, folding gently until well combined, and it will make ribbons when you lift your spoon out.
4. Put the mix into a piping bag and create 1.5-inch rounds on a lined baking sheet.
5. Tap pan against the counter a few times to release air bubbles. Then, let sit for 30 minutes to an hour to become dry. Bake for 10-12 minutes. Allow to cool on wire racks.
6. Assemble with chocolate cream filling.

PB&J Macarons

Ingredients

- Powdered sugar (1 c.)
- Egg whites (2, room temperature)
- Granulated sugar (3 Tbsp.)
- Vanilla extract (0.5 tsp.)
- Peanuts (0.25 c., roasted, unsalted)
- Almond flour (0.25 c.)
- Jam of choice for filling (0.25 c.)

Instructions

1. Prepare two baking sheets with parchment paper. Then, grind up your peanuts in a blender or processor until fine. Mix in the almond flour and sugar into ground peanuts. Pulse to create a fine powder, the texture of flour. Sift through a sieve and discard any chunks that don't go through.
2. In a bowl, beat egg whites until they begin to foam. Then, add in sugar until you get soft peaks. Mix in vanilla and beat until peaks stiffen.
3. Take peanut mixture and fold gently into the eggs until well incorporated.
4. Place in a piping bag and create 1.5-inch circles roughly 1 inch apart. Then, tap sheet on counter to eliminate air bubbles. Let sit for 30 minutes to an hour to get a crust on top.
5. Bake at 375F for 13-15 minutes, then remove parchment paper from pan to rest on rack to cool. Remove macarons from parchment and spread jam across one side, sandwiching with another. Eat within the same day for best results.

Peanut Butter and Honey Macarons

Ingredients

- Peanut Macaron Recipe
- Peanut butter and honey buttercream

For peanut butter and honey buttercream:

- Butter (0.25 c. butter, softened)
- Peanut butter (0.5 c.)
- Honey (2 Tbsp.)
- Powdered sugar (2 c.)
- Milk (1 Tbsp.)

Instructions

1. Prepare Peanut Macaron recipe
2. Prepare buttercream. To do so, throw all ingredients into a bowl and beat until smooth. If thick, add a touch of milk, and if too thin, add a touch of powdered sugar.
3. Pipe buttercream into peanut macarons.

Chocolate Nutella Macarons

Ingredients

- Classic Chocolate Macaron recipe
- Nutella buttercream

For Nutella buttercream:

- Butter (4 Tbsp., unsalted)
- Nutella (0.33 c.)
- Powdered sugar (2 c.)
- Salt (pinch)
- Milk (as needed)

Instructions

1. Prepare cookies according to Classic Chocolate macaron recipe.
2. Prepare your buttercream. Begin with butter in a bowl, creaming it. Then, combine in the Nutella until well mixed. Sift in powdered sugar and a pinch of salt while mixing on low until well incorporated.
3. Boost speed to medium-high and beat until thick and creamy. If necessary, add milk to thin, or add sugar to thicken.
4. Assemble macarons with buttercream piped into them.

Pecan Pie Macarons

Ingredients

- Classic Vanilla Macaron Recipe
- Pecan pie filling

For pecan pie filling:

- Brandy or cognac (2 tsp—optional)
- Dulce de leche (14-ounce can)
- Pecans (0.66 c., chopped)

Instructions

1. Prepare macarons according to instructions.
2. Create pecan pie filling. Take dulce de leche and mix it with the pecan pieces. Combine with alcohol if you are using it.
3. Place a Tbsp. of mixture onto the center of the bottom of macaron and top with a second macaron.
4. Let sit in fridge to firm up. Remove 30 minutes prior to serving and consume within 3-4 days.

Maple Walnut Macarons

Ingredients

- Egg whites (3 large, at room temperature)
- Maple extract (2 tsp)
- Powdered sugar (1.5 c.)
- Vanilla extract (0.5 tsp)
- Walnuts (1 c.)
- Maple walnut buttercream

For the maple walnut buttercream:

- Butter (1 stick, room temperature)
- Maple extract (2 tsp)
- Maple syrup (0.25 c.)
- Powdered sugar (3 c.)
- Vanilla extract (1 tsp)
- Walnuts (1 c., ground)

Instructions

1. Warm oven to 280F and prepare two baking sheets with parchment.
2. In a processor, grind down your walnuts. Measure out 0.66 c., then mix that with powdered sugar. Set aside the remainder of ground walnuts for later. Then, process longer until you have a fine powder. Sift powder, discarding chunks stuck in a sieve.
3. Beat egg whites until they froth, then mix sugar into them until incorporated, Tbsp. by Tbsp., then beat eggs to stiff peaks. Mix in extracts.

4. Fold in half of your walnut mixture until well combined, then add in the second half until it begins to ribbon.
5. Put batter into your pastry bag. Create 1.5-inch cookies, spaced 1 inch apart. Then tap baking sheet on the countertop to settle the batter and release air bubbles.
6. Let macarons sit for up to an hour until the top is no longer sticky or wet.
7. Bake for 15-18 minutes, rotating halfway through. Tops should be hard, but not browning. Let cool.
8. Prepare maple walnut buttercream. Grind down walnuts, so you have 1 c. of crushed and powdered nuts. Cream butter, then add in maple syrup and powdered sugar bit by bit until you achieve the right texture, then add in extracts.
9. Fold in nuts to the mixture and put it into a piping bag. Pipe into macarons and serve.

White Chocolate Macadamia Nut Macarons

Ingredients

- Classic Vanilla Macaron recipe
- White chocolate macadamia ganache

For the ganache

- White chocolate (7 oz.)
- Heavy cream (0.33 c.)
- Ground macadamia nuts (0.5 c.)

Instructions

1. Prepare macarons according to recipe.
2. To create your ganache, chop up your chocolate and put it into a bowl. It needs to be high quality and cut into very small pieces.
3. Warm cream in a saucepan without boiling it. Dump the cream atop the chocolate and let it melt. Stir to immerse well after a minute or two. Once melted, toss in the nuts and stir again. Let rest to room temperature and then refrigerate for 30 minutes before you use it.
4. Pipe it onto macarons. If too tough to pipe, then warm it up in the microwave for just a few seconds. If it is too thin, refrigerate it a bit longer.

Chapter 4: Coffee, Matcha, and Other Drink Macarons

Classic Coffee Macarons

Ingredients

- Almond flour (1 c.)
- Egg whites (3, room temperature)
- Granulated sugar (0.25 c.)
- Instant coffee (1 Tbsp.)
- Powdered sugar (2 c.)

Instructions

1. Beat egg whites until they begin to peak. Then, mix in granulated sugar until stiff peaks form.
2. Sift almond flour and powdered sugar, then sift the coffee powder into a bowl. Combine sifted ingredients then stir them into your egg whites. Carefully avoid overmixing. Wait until well combined, then place into a piping bag.
3. Pipe onto parchment-lined baking sheet roughly an inch apart, making 1.5-inch rounds. Tap sheet on the counter a few times per side to eliminate air bubbles, then leave macarons to sit on the counter to harden, between 30 minutes and an hour.
4. Bake at 300F for about 12 minutes. They're done when they release from paper and are firm to the touch, but not yet browning.
5. Cool, then fill macarons with Classic Coffee Filling (See next recipe)

Classic Coffee Filling

Ingredients

- Chocolate chips (1 c.)
- Heavy whipping cream (0.5 c.)
- Instant coffee (1 Tbsp.)

Instructions

1. Place chocolate chips and coffee together. Then, in a thick pot, warm heavy cream up to nearly boiling, but not quite. Then, pour it into the chocolate chips, whisking well until it is melted. Allow it to cool and thicken before using.
2. Spread onto macarons when thick enough to not run.

Classic Matcha Macarons

Ingredients

- Almond flour (0.75 c.)
- Egg whites (3)
- Granulated sugar (0.75 c.)
- Matcha (1 Tbsp.)
- Powdered sugar (1 c.)
- Cream cheese filling

Cream cheese filling:

- Cream cheese (0.75 c., room temperature)
- Milk (1 Tbsp.)
- Powdered sugar (1.5 c.)

Instructions

1. Prepare egg whites, beating them until they begin to form soft peaks. Then, mix in half of the granulated sugar until peaks stiffen. Add last half of granulated sugar and beat until shiny, fluffy, and stiff.
2. Sift out powdered sugar, almond flour, and matcha into the egg whites and fold gently until well combined.
3. Warm oven to 300F.
4. Place batter into a piping bag and create 1.5-inch macarons on a parchment-lined baking sheet. Tap pan on counter several times to get rid of air bubbles, then let rest on counter for up to an hour to form a skin on the cookies.
5. Bake for 15 minutes, then let rest until cool.
6. Prepare cream cheese filling. Combine powdered sugar, cheese, and milk and beat until smooth and fluffy. Place it into a piping bag.
7. Fill macarons with cream cheese mixture and sandwich together.

Vanilla Macchiato Macarons

Ingredients

- Classic Coffee Macarons Recipe
- Classic Vanilla Buttercream Recipe

Instructions

1. Prepare Classic Coffee Macarons, following the recipe instructions.
2. Prepare Classic Vanilla Buttercream, following the recipe instructions.
3. Assemble with buttercream on sides of cookies, then press together.
4. Optional—dust with cocoa powder for garnish.

Coffee Caramel Macarons

Ingredients

- Classic Coffee Macarons recipe
- Cinnamon Caramel Buttercream

For cinnamon caramel buttercream:

- Butter (7 Tbsp.)
- Ground cinnamon (0.5 tsp)
- Powdered sugar (1.33 c.)
- Salted caramel sauce (2 Tbsp.)

Instructions

1. Prepare your macarons according to the Classic Coffee Macarons recipe.
2. While macarons cook, prepare your cinnamon caramel buttercream. To do so, place all ingredients into a bowl and whip together until it becomes thick and fluffy. If it is too loose, place it in the fridge for a few minutes.
3. Assemble cookies, piping a dollop in the center of one macaron before topping it with another. Refrigerate overnight before serving for best taste.

Espresso Mocha Macarons

Ingredients

- Classic Coffee Macarons recipe (omit half of instant coffee powder and substitute it for cocoa powder)
- Dark chocolate buttercream

For dark chocolate buttercream:

- Butter (0.5 c.)
- Powdered sugar (3 c.)
- Cocoa powder (4 Tbsp.)
- Dark chocolate cocoa powder (3 Tbsp.)
- Heavy cream (3 Tbsp.)
- Sea salt (1 tsp)

Instructions

1. Prepare Classic Coffee Macarons recipe, leaving out half of the instant coffee powder and replacing it with cocoa powder for a chocolatey taste. Otherwise, complete as normal.
2. As macarons bake, prepare your buttercream. Cream together your butter and sugar until you have a fluffy mix. Then, toss in the cocoa powders and cream. Beat well until it becomes creamy and loses the graininess. Mix in the sea salt.
3. Place buttercream into piping bag and pipe into the center of one macaron, topping it with the second.

Hazelnut Coffee Macarons

Ingredients

- Classic Coffee Macarons recipe
- Nutella ganache

For the Nutella ganache:

- Dark chocolate (0.75 c.)
- Heavy cream (0.5 c.)
- Nutella (3 Tbsp.)

Instructions

1. Prepare your coffee macarons according to the recipe without any alterations.
2. While macarons bake, begin assembling your Nutella ganache. To do so, warm your cream to just before boiling. Then, mix the chocolate into the cream until melted. Then, mix in the Nutella as well, blending well.
3. Leave ganache in the fridge for a few hours to firm up. Then, pipe or spoon filling onto half of macaron, topping with a second.
4. Let firm up in the fridge and enjoy.

Matcha Mango Macarons

Ingredients

- Classic Matcha Macaron recipe
- Mango Buttercream recipe (See Chapter 7)

Instructions

1. Prepare matcha macarons according to recipe without any alterations.
2. While matcha macarons bake, create the mango buttercream according to the recipe without any alterations.
3. When macarons are cooled, fill with buttercream. Refrigerate to set.

Matcha Raspberry Macarons

Ingredients

- Classic Matcha Macaron recipe
- Raspberry buttercream

For the raspberry buttercream

- Butter (0.5 c. unsalted, room temperature)
- Granulated sugar (1 Tbsp.)
- Mashed raspberries (0.5 c. fresh or frozen, measure after mashing)
- Powdered sugar (2 c., sifted)
- Salt (0.25 tsp)
- Vanilla extract (0.5 tsp)

Instructions

1. Prepare macarons according to instructions.
2. Prepare your raspberry buttercream. Take a small bowl and combine the mashed raspberries with granulated sugar. Allow it to sit for 30 minutes to macerate. Then, strain through a sieve to get the juices out, discarding the seeds and fruit.
3. Take a stand mixer and put in your butter. Cream it, then sift in the powdered sugar. Mix at low until sugar is moist and starting to cream, then raise the speed, adding in the juice and extract. Finally, add in the salt and beat until frosting is fluffy and light. Transfer it into a pastry bag and refrigerate until you are ready to use it.
4. To assemble, take macaron, coat half with buttercream, then top with a second macaron.

Thai Tea Macarons

Ingredients

- Classic Vanilla Macarons recipe—omit vanilla.
- Thai tea ganache

For the Thai tea ganache:

- White chocolate (3 c., chopped)
- Heavy cream (1 c.)
- Thai tea leaves

Instructions

1. Prepare macarons according to Classic Vanilla macarons recipe, omitting the vanilla. Use an orange or copper colored food coloring and follow all other instructions.
2. Create your ganache. Warm the cream until hot but not boiling in the microwave or stovetop. Then, add in the tea leaves to the cream to let it soak and impart flavor.
3. While the tea is steeping, roughly chop up the white chocolate into small bits and set it into a large bowl.
4. Strain your cream, discard the leaves, and pour the cream into the chocolate, leaving it to sit for a minute and then stir it together to combine melted chocolate.
5. Let ganache cool on the counter until no longer hot to the touch, then place in the refrigerator to harden.
6. Take out of fridge, mix together, and use to fill your macarons.

Pumpkin Spice Latte Macarons

Ingredients

- Almond flour (1 c.)
- Cream of tartar (0.25 tsp)
- Egg whites (3 large)
- Food coloring gel (3-5 drops, orange preferably—optional)
- Granulated sugar (0.25 c.)
- Instant espresso powder (1 tsp)
- Powdered sugar (1.33 c.)
- Pumpkin pie spice (1 tsp)
- Salt (pinch)
- Espresso filling (or Classic Coffee Filling recipe if you prefer to avoid uncooked egg whites)

For espresso filling

- Egg whites (4)
- Instant espresso powder (0.5 tsp)
- Sugar (0.5 c.)

Instructions

1. Begin setting up your two sheet pans with paper.
2. Take a food processor and combine almond flour, espresso powder, powdered sugar, and pumpkin spice. Pulse in processor a few times, then sift well. You should get less than 2 Tbsp. of almond left behind by the time that it is done.

3. Take egg whites and combine them with salt, sugar, and cream of tartar. Whip together until it begins to form stiff peaks. Then, add in your coloring if you plan to use it.
4. Combine the dried ingredients into the mixture with a spatula, careful not to overmix. Fold gently until you have a shiny, smooth mixture. A spoonful of batter should peak, then quickly relax.
5. Move mixture into a pastry bag, then create cookies. They should be 1.5-inch in diameter and roughly 1 inch apart. When all cookies are put out onto plates, tap rapidly against the counter to release bubbles. Let macarons sit for an hour to create a crust across the top. They should not be sticky if you touch them.
6. Warm oven to 300 F and bake for between 15 and 20 minutes, until the shell is hard, but it has not started to brown. Cool, then remove from parchment.
7. Prepare your coffee filling now. Take an electric mixer and whip up your egg whites until they begin to stiffen up. Then, slowly incorporate the sugar and espresso into the whites until you have stiff peaks. If you dislike the idea of using uncooked egg whites for your filling, you can substitute this out for the Classic Coffee Filling recipe at the beginning of the chapter.

Spiced Chai Macarons

Ingredients

- Almond flour (1 c.)
- Cinnamon (0.25 tsp)
- Cloves (0.125 tsp)
- Cream of tartar (0.25 tsp)
- Egg whites (2 large)
- Ginger (0.125 tsp)
- Granulated sugar (0.25 c.)
- Nutmeg (0.125 tsp)
- Powdered sugar (0.75 c.)
- Vanilla extract (0.25 tsp)
- Classic Vanilla Buttercream recipe

Instructions

1. Sift together your almond flour and powdered sugar at least twice, removing any chunks.

2. Beat eggs in stand mixer bowl until they begin to froth. Then, combine in the cream of tartar with the sugar. Create thick, stiff peaks. Then, mix in the spices and vanilla extract, continuing on low until everything is well-incorporated.

3. Sift together almond flour and powdered sugar into the egg mix. Gently fold together batter until well combined, but not overmixed.

4. Move batter into a pastry bag and pipe onto a baking sheet lined with parchment paper. Tap pan against the counter several times to release bubbles, then let sit for an hour before you bake.

5. Cook for 17 minutes at 300F. They should be easily removable from the tray, but not browning, when done. Cool for 10 minutes, then transfer to tray.

Create Classic Vanilla Buttercream recipe, then fill cooled macarons, taking the cookies and piping along the flat side, then sandwiching it together with a second cookie. Let set in fridge overnight

PART II

Smoothie Diet Recipes

The smoothie diet is all about replacing some of your meals with smoothies that are loaded with veggies and fruits. It has been found that the smoothie diet is very helpful in losing weight along with excess fat. The ingredients of the smoothies will vary, but they will focus mainly on vegetables and fruits. The best part about the smoothie diet is that there is no need to count your calorie intake and less food tracking. The diet is very low in calories and is also loaded with phytonutrients.

Apart from weight loss, there are various other benefits of the smoothie diet. It can help you to stay full for a longer time as most smoothies are rich in fiber. It can also help you to control your cravings as smoothies are full of flavor and nutrients. Whenever you feel like snacking, just prepare a smoothie, and you are good to go. Also, smoothies can aid in digestion as they are rich in important minerals and vitamins. Fruits such as mango are rich in carotenoids that can help in improving your skin quality. As the smoothie diet is mainly based on veggies and fruits, it can detoxify your body.

In this section, you will find various recipes of smoothies that you can include in your smoothie diet.

Chapter 1: Fruit Smoothies

The best way of having fruits is by making smoothies. Fruit smoothies can help you start your day with loads of nutrients so that you can remain energetic throughout the day. Here are some easy-to-make fruit smoothie recipes that you can enjoy during any time of the day.

Quick Fruit Smoothie

Total Prep & Cooking Time: Fifteen minutes

Yields: Four servings

Nutrition Facts: Calories: 115.2 | Protein: 1.2g | Carbs: 27.2g | Fat: 0.5g | Fiber: 3.6g

Ingredients

- One cup of strawberries
- One banana (cut in chunks)
- Two peaches
- Two cups of ice
- One cup of orange and mango juice

Method:

1. Add banana, strawberries, and peaches in a blender.
2. Blend until frothy and smooth.
3. Add the orange and mango juice and blend again. Add ice for adjusting the consistency and blend for two minutes.
4. Divide the smoothie in glasses and serve with mango chunks from the top.

Triple Threat Smoothie

Total Prep & Cooking Time: Ten minutes

Yields: Four servings

Nutrition Facts: Calories: 132.2 | Protein: 3.4g | Carbs: 27.6g | Fat: 1.3g | Fiber: 2.7g

Ingredients

- One kiwi (sliced)
- One banana (chopped)
- One cup of each
    - Ice cubes
    - Strawberries
- Half cup of blueberries
- One-third cup of orange juice
- Eight ounces of peach yogurt

Method:

1. Add kiwi, strawberries, and bananas in a food processor.
2. Blend until smooth.
3. Add the blueberries along with orange juice. Blend again for two minutes.
4. Add peach yogurt and ice cubes. Give it a pulse.
5. Pour the prepared smoothie in smoothie glasses and serve with blueberry chunks from the top.

Tropical Smoothie

Total Prep & Cooking Time: Fifteen minutes

Yields: Two servings

Nutrition Facts: Calories: 127.3 | Protein: 1.6g | Carbs: 30.5g | Fat: 0.7g | Fiber: 4.2g

Ingredients

- One mango (seeded)
- One papaya (cubed)
- Half cup of strawberries
- One-third cup of orange juice
- Five ice cubes

Method:

1. Add mango, strawberries, and papaya in a blender. Blend the ingredients until smooth.
2. Add ice cubes and orange juice for adjusting the consistency.
3. Blend again.
4. Serve with strawberry chunks from the top.

Fruit and Mint Smoothie

Total Prep & Cooking Time: Fifteen minutes

Yields: Two servings

Nutrition Facts: Calories: 90.3 | Protein: 0.7g | Carbs: 21.4g | Fat: 0.4g | Fiber: 2.5g

Ingredients

- One-fourth cup of each
    - Applesauce (unsweetened)
    - Red grapes (seedless, frozen)
- One tbsp. of lime juice
- Three strawberries (frozen)
- One cup of pineapple cubes
- Three mint leaves

Method:

1. Add grapes, lime juice, and applesauce in a blender. Blend the ingredients until frothy and smooth.

2. Add pineapple cubes, mint leaves, and frozen strawberries in the blender. Pulse the ingredients for a few times until the pineapple and strawberries are crushed.

3. Serve with mint leaves from the top.

Banana Smoothie

Total Prep & Cooking Time: Ten minutes

Yields: Four servings

Nutrition Facts: Calories: 122.6 | Protein: 1.3g | Carbs: 34.6g | Fat: 0.4g | Fiber: 2.2g

Ingredients

- Three bananas (sliced)
- One cup of fresh pineapple juice
- One tbsp. of honey
- Eight cubes of ice

Method:

1. Combine the bananas and pineapple juice in a blender.
2. Blend until smooth.
3. Add ice cubes along with honey.
4. Blend for two minutes.
5. Serve immediately.

Dragon Fruit Smoothie

Total Prep & Cooking Time: Twenty minutes

Yields: Four servings

Nutrition Facts: Calories: 147.6 | Protein: 5.2g | Carbs: 21.4g | Fat: 6.4g | Fiber: 2.9g

Ingredients

- One-fourth cup of almonds
- Two tbsps. of shredded coconut
- One tsp. of chocolate chips
- One cup of yogurt
- One dragon fruit (chopped)
- Half cup of pineapple cubes
- One tbsp. of honey

Method:

1. Add almonds, dragon fruit, coconut, and chocolate chips in a high power blender. Blend until smooth.
2. Add yogurt, pineapple, and honey. Blend well.
3. Serve with chunks of dragon fruit from the top.

Kefir Blueberry Smoothie

Total Prep & Cooking Time: Fifteen minutes

Yields: Two servings

Nutrition Facts: Calories: 304.2 | Protein: 7.3g | Carbs: 41.3g | Fat: 13.2g | Fiber: 4.6g

Ingredients

- Half cup of kefir
- One cup of blueberries (frozen)
- Half banana (cubed)

- One tbsp. of almond butter
- Two tsps. of honey

Method:

1. Add blueberries, banana cubes, and kefir in a blender.
2. Blend until smooth.
3. Add honey and almond butter.
4. Pulse the smoothie for a few times.
5. Serve immediately.

Ginger Fruit Smoothie

Total Prep & Cooking Time: Fifteen minutes

Yields: Two servings

Nutrition Facts: Calories: 160.2 | Protein: 1.9g | Carbs: 41.3g | Fat: 0.7g | Fiber: 5.6g

Ingredients

- One-fourth cup of each
    - Blueberries (frozen)
    - Green grapes (seedless)
- Half cup of green apple (chopped)
- One cup of water
- Three strawberries
- One piece of ginger
- One tbsp. of agave nectar

Method:

1. Add blueberries, grapes, and water in a blender. Blend the ingredients.
2. Add green apple, strawberries, agave nectar, and ginger. Blend for making thick slushy.
3. Serve immediately.

Fruit Batido

Total Prep & Cooking Time: Fifteen minutes

Yields: Six servings

Nutrition Facts: Calories: 129.3 | Protein: 4.2g | Carbs: 17.6g | Fat: 4.6g | Fiber: 0.6g

Ingredients

- One can of evaporated milk
- One cup of papaya (chopped)
- One-fourth cup of white sugar
- One tsp. of vanilla extract
- One tsp. of cinnamon (ground)
- One tray of ice cubes

Method:

1. Add papaya, white sugar, cinnamon, and vanilla extract in a food processor. Blend the ingredients until smooth.
2. Add milk and ice cubes. Blend for making slushy.
3. Serve immediately.

Banana Peanut Butter Smoothie

Total Prep & Cooking Time: Ten minutes

Yields: Four servings

Nutrition Facts: Calories: 332 | Protein: 13.2g | Carbs: 35.3g | Fat: 17.8g | Fiber: 3.9g

Ingredients

- Two bananas (cubed)
- Two cups of milk
- Half cup of peanut butter
- Two tbsps. of honey
- Two cups of ice cubes

Method:

1. Add banana cubes and peanut butter in a blender. Blend for making a smooth paste.
2. Add milk, ice cubes, and honey. Blend the ingredients until smooth.
3. Serve with banana chunks from the top.

Chapter 2: Breakfast Smoothies

Smoothie forms an essential part of breakfast in the smoothie diet plan. Here are some breakfast smoothie recipes for you that can be included in your daily breakfast plan.

Berry Banana Smoothie

Total Prep & Cooking Time: Twenty minutes

Yields: Two servings

Nutrition Facts: Calories: 330 | Protein: 6.7g | Carbs: 56.3g | Fat: 13.2g | Fiber: 5.5g

Ingredients

- One cup of each
    - Strawberries
    - Peaches (cubed)
    - Apples (cubed)
- One banana (cubed)
- Two cups of vanilla ice cream
- Half cup of ice cubes
- One-third cup of milk

Method:

1. Place strawberries, peaches, banana, and apples in a blender. Pulse the ingredients.
2. Add milk, ice cream, and ice cubes. Blend the smoothie until frothy and smooth.
3. Serve with a scoop of ice cream from the top.

Berry Surprise

Total Prep & Cooking Time: Ten minutes

Yields: Two servings

Nutrition Facts: Calories: 164.2 | Protein: 1.2g | Carbs: 40.2g | Fat: 0.4g | Fiber: 4.8g

Ingredients

- One cup of strawberries
- Half cup of pineapple cubes
- One-third cup of raspberries
- Two tbsps. of limeade concentrate (frozen)

Method:

1. Combine pineapple cubes, strawberries, and raspberries in a food processor. Blend the ingredients until smooth.
2. Add the frozen limeade and blend again.
3. Divide the smoothie in glasses and serve immediately.

Coconut Matcha Smoothie

Total Prep & Cooking Time: Twenty minutes

Yields: Two servings

Nutrition Facts: Calories: 362 | Protein: 7.2g | Carbs: 70.1g | Fat: 8.7g | Fiber: 12.1g

Ingredients

- One large banana
- One cup of frozen mango cubes
- Two leaves of kale (torn)
- Three tbsps. of white beans (drained)
- Two tbsps. of shredded coconut (unsweetened)
- Half tsp. of matcha green tea (powder)
- Half cup of water

Method:

1. Add cubes of mango, banana, white beans, and kale in a blender. Blend all the ingredients until frothy and smooth.
2. Add shredded coconut, white beans, water, and green tea powder. Blend for thirty seconds.
3. Serve with shredded coconut from the top.

Cantaloupe Frenzy

Total Prep & Cooking Time: Ten minutes

Yields: Three servings

Nutrition Facts: Calories: 108.3 | Protein: 1.6g | Carbs: 26.2g | Fat: 0.2g | Fiber: 1.6g

Ingredients

- One cantaloupe (seeded, chopped)
- Three tbsps. of white sugar
- Two cups of ice cubes

Method:

1. Place the chopped cantaloupe along with white sugar in a blender. Puree the mixture.
2. Add cubes of ice and blend again.
3. Pour the smoothie in serving glasses. Serve immediately.

Berry Lemon Smoothie

Total Prep & Cooking Time: Ten minutes

Yields: Four servings

Nutrition Facts: Calories: 97.2 | Protein: 5.4g | Carbs: 19.4g | Fat: 0.4g | Fiber: 1.8g

Ingredients

- Eight ounces of blueberry yogurt
- One and a half cup of milk (skim)
- One cup of ice cubes
- Half cup of blueberries
- One-third cup of strawberries
- One tsp. of lemonade mix

Method:

1. Add blueberry yogurt, skim milk, blueberries, and strawberries in a food processor. Blend the ingredients until smooth.
2. Add lemonade mix and ice cubes. Pulse the mixture for making a creamy and smooth smoothie.
3. Divide the smoothie in glasses and serve.

Orange Glorious

Total Prep & Cooking Time: Ten minutes

Yields: Four servings

Nutrition Facts: Calories: 212 | Protein: 3.4g | Carbs: 47.3g | Fat: 1.5g | Fiber: 0.5g

Ingredients

- Six ounces of orange juice concentrate (frozen)
- One cup of each
    - Water
    - Milk
- Half cup of white sugar
- Twelve ice cubes
- One tsp. of vanilla extract

Method:

1. Combine orange juice concentrate, white sugar, milk, and water in a blender.
2. Add vanilla extract and ice cubes. Blend the mixture until smooth.
3. Pour the smoothie in glasses and enjoy!

Grapefruit Smoothie

Total Prep & Cooking Time: Ten minutes

Yields: Two servings

Nutrition Facts: Calories: 200.3 | Protein: 4.7g | Carbs: 46.3g | Fat: 1.2g | Fiber: 7.6g

Ingredients

- Three grapefruits (peeled)
- One cup of water
- Three ounces of spinach
- Six ice cubes
- Half-inch piece of ginger
- One tsp. of flax seeds

Method:

1. Combine spinach, grapefruit, and ginger in a high power blender. Blend until smooth.

2. Add water, flax seeds, and ice cubes. Blend smooth.

3. Pour the smoothie in glasses and serve.

Sour Smoothie

Total Prep & Cooking Time: Ten minutes

Yields: Two servings

Nutrition Facts: Calories: 102.6 | Protein: 2.3g | Carbs: 30.2g | Fat: 0.7g | Fiber: 7.9g

Ingredients

- One cup of ice cubes
- Two fruit limes (peeled)
- One orange (peeled)
- One lemon (peeled)
- One kiwi (peeled)
- One tsp. of honey

Method:

1. Add fruit limes, lemon, orange, and kiwi in a food processor. Blend until frothy and smooth.
2. Add cubes of ice and honey. Pulse the ingredients.
3. Divide the smoothie in glasses and enjoy!

Ginger Orange Smoothie

Total Prep & Cooking Time: Ten minutes

Yields: One serving

Nutrition Facts: Calories: 115.6 | Protein: 2.2g | Carbs: 27.6g | Fat: 1.3g | Fiber: 5.7g

Ingredients

- One large orange
- Two carrots (peeled, cut in chunks)
- Half cup of each
    - Red grapes
    - Ice cubes
- One-fourth cup of water
- One-inch piece of ginger

Method:

1. Combine carrots, grapes, and orange in a high power blender. Blend until frothy and smooth.

2. Add ice cubes, ginger, and water. Blend the ingredients for thirty seconds.

3. Serve immediately.

Cranberry Smoothie

Total Prep & Cooking Time: One hour and ten minutes

Yields: Two servings

Nutrition Facts: Calories: 155.9 | Protein: 2.2g | Carbs: 33.8g | Fat: 1.6g | Fiber: 5.2g

Ingredients

- One cup of almond milk
- Half cup of mixed berries (frozen)
- One-third cup of cranberries
- One banana

Method:

1. Blend mixed berries, banana, and cranberries in a high power food processor. Blend until smooth.
2. Add almond milk and blend again for twenty seconds.
3. Refrigerate the prepared smoothie for one hour.
4. Serve chilled.

Creamsicle Smoothie

Total Prep & Cooking Time: Ten minutes

Yields: Two servings

Nutrition Facts: Calories: 121.3 | Protein: 4.7g | Carbs: 19.8g | Fat: 2.5g | Fiber: 0.3g

Ingredients

- One cup of orange juice
- One and a half cup of crushed ice
- Half cup of milk
- One tsp. of white sugar

Method:

1. Blend milk, orange juice, white sugar, and ice in a high power blender.
2. Keep blending until there is no large chunk of ice. Try to keep the consistency of slushy.
3. Serve immediately.

Sunshine Smoothie

Total Prep & Cooking Time: Thirty minutes

Yields: Four servings

Nutrition Facts: Calories: 176.8 | Protein: 4.2g | Carbs: 39.9g | Fat: 1.3g | Fiber: 3.9g

Ingredients

- Two nectarines (pitted, quartered)
- One banana (cut in chunks)
- One orange (peeled, quartered)
- One cup of vanilla yogurt
- One-third cup of orange juice
- One tbsp. of honey

Method:

1. Add banana chunks, nectarines, and orange in a blender. Blender for two minutes.

2. Add vanilla yogurt, honey, and orange juice. Blend the ingredients until frothy and smooth.

3. Pour the smoothie in glasses and serve.

Chapter 3: Vegetable Smoothies

Apart from fruit smoothies, vegetable smoothies can also provide you with essential nutrients. In fact, vegetable smoothies are tasty as well. So, here are some vegetable smoothie recipes for you.

Mango Kale Berry Smoothie

Total Prep & Cooking Time: Ten minutes

Yields: Four servings

Nutrition Facts: Calories: 117.3 | Protein: 3.1g | Carbs: 22.6g | Fat: 3.6g | Fiber: 6.2g

Ingredients

- One cup of orange juice
- One-third cup of kale
- One and a half cup of mixed berries (frozen)
- Half cup of mango chunks
- One-fourth cup of water
- Two tbsps. of chia seeds

Method:

1. Take a high power blender and add kale, orange juice, berries, mango chunks, chia seeds, and half a cup of water.
2. Blend the ingredients on high settings until smooth.
3. In case the smoothie is very thick, you can adjust the consistency by adding more water.
4. Pour the smoothie in glasses and serve.

Breakfast Pink Smoothie

Total Prep & Cooking Time: Ten minutes

Yields: Two servings

Nutrition Facts: Calories: 198.3 | Protein: 12.3g | Carbs: 6.3g | Fat: 4.5g | Fiber: 8.8g

Ingredients

- One and a half cup of strawberries (frozen)
- One cup of raspberries
- One orange (peeled)

- Two carrots
- Two cups of coconut milk (light)
- One small beet (quartered)

Method:

1. Add strawberries, raspberries, and orange in a blender. Blend until frothy and smooth.

2. Add beet, carrots, and coconut milk.

3. Blend again for one minute.

4. Divide the smoothie in glasses and serve.

Butternut Squash Smoothie

Total Prep & Cooking Time: Five minutes

Yields: Four servings

Nutrition Facts: Calories: 127.3 | Protein: 2.3g | Carbs: 32.1g | Fat: 1.2g | Fiber: 0.6g

Ingredients

- Two cups of almond milk
- One-fourth cup of nut butter (of your choice)
- One cup of water
- One and a half cup of butternut squash (frozen)
- Two ripe bananas
- One tsp. of cinnamon (ground)
- Two tbsps. of hemp protein
- Half cup of strawberries
- One tbsp. of chia seeds
- Half tbsp. of bee pollen

Method:

1. Add butternut squash, bananas, strawberries, and almond milk in a blender. Blend until frothy and smooth.

2. Add water, nut butter, cinnamon, hemp protein, chia seeds, and bee pollen. Blend the ingredients f0r two minutes.

3. Divide the smoothie in glasses and enjoy!

Zucchini and Wild Blueberry Smoothie

Total Prep & Cooking Time: Ten minutes

Yields: Three servings

Nutrition Facts: Calories: 190.2 | Protein: 7.3g | Carbs: 27.6g | Fat: 8.1g | Fiber: 5.7g

Ingredients

- One banana
- One cup of wild blueberries (frozen)
- One-fourth cup of peas (frozen)
- Half cup of zucchini (frozen, chopped)
- One tbsp. of each
    - Hemp hearts
    - Chia seeds
    - Bee pollen
- One-third cup of almond milk
- Two tbsps. of nut butter (of your choice)
- Ten cubes of ice

Method:

1. Add blueberries, banana, peas, and zucchini in a high power blender. Blend the ingredients for two minutes.
2. Add chia seeds, hemp hearts, almond milk, bee pollen, nut butter, and ice. Blend the mixture for making a thick and smooth smoothie.
3. Pour the smoothie in glasses and serve with chopped blueberries from the top.

Cauliflower and Blueberry Smoothie

Total Prep & Cooking Time: Five minutes

Yields: Two servings

Nutrition Facts: Calories: 201.9 | Protein: 7.1g | Carbs: 32.9g | Fat: 10.3g | Fiber: 4.6g

Ingredients

- One Clementine (peeled)
- Three-fourth cup of cauliflower (frozen)
- Half cup of wild blueberries (frozen)
- One cup of Greek yogurt
- One tbsp. of peanut butter
- Bunch of spinach

Method:

1. Add cauliflower, Clementine, and blueberries in a blender. Blend for one minute.

2. Add peanut butter, spinach, and yogurt. Pulse the ingredients for two minutes until smooth.

3. Divide the prepared smoothie in glasses and enjoy!

Immunity Booster Smoothie

Total Prep & Cooking Time: Ten minutes

Yields: Two servings

Nutrition Facts: Calories: 301.9 | Protein: 5.4g | Carbs: 70.7g | Fat: 4.3g | Fiber:

8.9g

Ingredients

For the orange layer:

- One persimmon (quartered)
- One ripe mango (chopped)
- One lime (juiced)
- One tbsp. of nut butter (of your choice)
- Half tsp. of turmeric powder
- One pinch of cayenne pepper
- One cup of coconut milk

For the pink layer:

- One small beet (cubed)
- One cup of berries (frozen)
- One pink grapefruit (quartered)
- One-fourth cup of pomegranate juice
- Half cup of water
- Six leaves of mint
- One tsp. of honey

Method:

1. Add the ingredients for the orange layer in a blender. Blend for making a smooth liquid.

2. Pour the orange liquid evenly in serving glasses.

3. Add the pink layer ingredients in a blender. Blend for making a smooth liquid.

4. Pour the pink liquid slowly over the orange layer.

5. Pour in such a way so that both layers can be differentiated.

6. Serve immediately.

Ginger, Carrot, and Turmeric Smoothie

Total Prep & Cooking Time: Forty minutes

Yields: Two servings

Nutrition Facts: Calories: 140 | Protein: 2.6g | Carbs: 30.2g | Fat: 2.2g | Fiber: 5.6g

Ingredients

For carrot juice:

- Two cups of water
- Two and a half cups of carrots

For smoothie:

- One ripe banana (sliced)
- One cup of pineapple (frozen, cubed)
- Half tbsp. of ginger
- One-fourth tsp. of turmeric (ground)
- Half cup of carrot juice
- One tbsp. of lemon juice
- One-third cup of almond milk

Method:

1. Add water and carrots in a high power blender. Blend on high settings for making smooth juice.

2. Take a dish towel and strain the juice over a bowl. Squeeze the towel for taking out most of the juice.

3. Add the ingredients for the smoothie in a blender and blend until frothy and creamy.

4. Add carrot juice and blend again.

5. Pour the smoothie in glasses and serve.

Romaine Mango Smoothie

Total Prep & Cooking Time: Five minutes

Yields: Two servings

Nutrition Facts: Calories: 117.3 | Protein: 2.6g | Carbs: 30.2g | Fat: 0.9g | Fiber: 4.2g

Ingredients

- Sixteen ounces of coconut water
- Two mangoes (pitted)
- One head of romaine (chopped)
- One banana
- One orange (peeled)
- Two cups of ice

Method:

1. Add mango, romaine, orange, and banana in a high power blender. Blend the ingredients until frothy and smooth.
2. Add coconut water and ice cubes. Blend for one minute.
3. Pour the prepared smoothie in glasses and serve.

Fig Zucchini Smoothie

Total Prep & Cooking Time: Ten minutes

Yields: Two servings

Nutrition Facts: Calories: 243.3 | Protein: 14.4g | Carbs: 74.3g | Fat: 27.6g | Fiber: 9.3g

Ingredients

- Half cup of cashew nuts
- One tsp. of cinnamon (ground)
- Two figs (halved)
- One banana
- Half tsp. of ginger (minced)
- One-third tsp. of honey
- One-fourth cup of ice cubes
- One pinch of salt
- Two tsps. of vanilla extract
- Three-fourth cup of water
- One cup of zucchini (chopped)

Method:

1. Add all the listed ingredients in a high power blender. Blend for two minutes until creamy and smooth.
2. Pour the smoothie in serving glasses and serve.

Carrot Peach Smoothie

Total Prep & Cooking Time: Ten minutes

Yields: Two servings

Nutrition Facts: Calories: 191.2 | Protein: 11.2g | Carbs: 34.6g | Fat: 2.7g | Fiber: 5.4g

Ingredients

- Two cups of peach
- One cup of baby carrots
- One banana (frozen)
- Two tbsps. of Greek yogurt
- One and a half cup of coconut water
- One tbsp. of honey

Method:

1. Add peach, baby carrots, and banana in a high power blender. Blend on high settings for one minute.//
2. Add Greek yogurt, honey, and coconut water. Give the mixture a whizz.
3. Pour the smoothie in glasses and serve.

Sweet Potato and Mango Smoothie

Total Prep & Cooking Time: Ten minutes

Yields: Two servings

Nutrition Facts: Calories: 133.3 | Protein: 3.6g | Carbs: 28.6g | Fat: 1.3g | Fiber: 6.2g

Ingredients

- One small sweet potato (cooked, smashed)
- Half cup of mango chunks (frozen)
- Two cups of coconut milk
- One tbsp. of chia seeds
- Two tsps. of maple syrup
- A handful of ice cubes

Method:

1. Add mango chunks and sweet potato in a high power blender. Blend until frothy and smooth.
2. Add chia seeds, coconut milk, ice cubes, and maple syrup. Blend again for one minute.
3. Divide the smoothie in glasses and serve.

Carrot Cake Smoothie

Total Prep & Cooking Time: Ten minutes

Yields: Two servings

Nutrition Facts: Calories: 289.3 | Protein: 3.6g | Carbs: 47.8g | Fat: 1.3g | Fiber: 0.6g

Ingredients

- One cup of carrots (chopped)
- One banana
- Half cup of almond milk
- One cup of Greek yogurt
- One tbsp. of maple syrup
- One tsp. of cinnamon (ground)
- One-fourth tsp. of nutmeg
- Half tsp. of ginger (ground)
- A handful of ice cubes

Method

1. Add banana, carrots, and almond milk in a blender. Blend until frothy and smooth.
2. Add yogurt, cinnamon, maple syrup, ginger, nutmeg, and ice cubes. Blend again for two minutes.
3. Divide the smoothie in serving glasses and serve.

Notes:

- You can add more ice cubes and turn the smoothie into slushy.
- You can store the leftover smoothie in the freezer for two days.

Chapter 4: Green Smoothies

Green smoothies can help in the process of detoxification as well as weight loss. Here are some easy-to-make green smoothie recipes for you.

Kale Avocado Smoothie

Total Prep & Cooking Time: Ten minutes

Yields: Two servings

Nutrition Facts: Calories: 401 | Protein: 11.2g | Carbs: 64.6g | Fat: 17.3g | Fiber: 10.2g

Ingredients

- One banana (cut in chunks)
- Half cup of blueberry yogurt
- One cup of kale (chopped)
- Half ripe avocado
- One-third cup of almond milk

Method:

1. Add blueberry, banana, avocado, and kale in a blender. Blend for making a smooth mixture.
2. Add the almond milk and blend again.
3. Divide the smoothie in glasses and serve.

Celery Pineapple Smoothie

Total Prep & Cooking Time: Ten minutes

Yields: Two servings

Nutrition Facts: Calories: 112 | Protein: 2.3g | Carbs: 3.6g | Fat: 1.2g | Fiber: 3.9g

Ingredients

- Three celery stalks (chopped)
- One cup of cubed pineapple
- One banana
- One pear
- Half cup of almond milk
- One tsp. of honey

Method:

1. Add celery stalks, pear, banana, and cubes of pineapple in a food processor. Blend until frothy and smooth.
2. Add honey and almond milk. Blend for two minutes.
3. Pour the smoothie in serving glasses and enjoy!

Cucumber Mango and Lime Smoothie

Total Prep & Cooking Time: Ten minutes

Yields: Two servings

Nutrition Facts: Calories: 165 | Protein: 2.2g | Carbs: 32.5g | Fat: 4.2g | Fiber: 3.7g

Ingredients

- One cup of ripe mango (frozen, cubed)
- Six cubes of ice
- Half cup of baby spinach leaves
- Two leaves of mint
- Two tsps. of lime juice
- Half cucumber (chopped)
- Three-fourth cup of coconut milk
- One-eighth tsp. of cayenne pepper

Method:

1. Add mango cubes, spinach leaves, and cucumber in a high power blender. Blend until frothy and smooth.
2. Add mint leaves, lime juice, coconut milk, cayenne pepper, and ice cubes. Process the ingredients until smooth.
3. Pour the smoothie in glasses and serve.

Kale, Melon, and Broccoli Smoothie

Total Prep & Cooking Time: Ten minutes

Yields: One serving

Nutrition Facts: Calories: 96.3 | Protein: 2.3g | Carbs: 24.3g | Fat: 1.2g | Fiber: 2.6g

Ingredients

- Eight ounces of honeydew melon
- One handful of kale
- Two ounces of broccoli florets
- One cup of coconut water
- Two sprigs of mint
- Two dates
- Half cup of lime juice
- Eight cubes of ice

Method:

1. Add kale, melon, and broccoli in a food processor. Whizz the ingredients for blending.

2. Add mint leaves and coconut water. Blend again.

3. Add lime juice, dates, and ice cubes. Blend the ingredients until smooth and creamy.

4. Pour the smoothie in a smoothie glass. Enjoy!

Kiwi Spinach Smoothie

Total Prep & Cooking Time: Ten minutes

Yields: Two servings

Nutrition Facts: Calories: 102 | Protein: 3.6g | Carbs: 21.3g | Fat: 2.2g | Fiber: 3.1g

Ingredients

- One kiwi (cut in chunks)
- One banana (cut in chunks)
- One cup of spinach leaves
- Three-fourth cup of almond milk
- One tbsp. of chia seeds
- Four cubes of ice

Method:

1. Add banana, kiwi, and spinach leaves in a blender. Blend the ingredients until smooth.
2. Add chia seeds, ice cubes, and almond milk. Blend again for one minute.
3. Pour the smoothie in serving glasses and serve.

Avocado Smoothie

Total Prep & Cooking Time: Ten minutes

Yields: Two servings

Nutrition Facts: Calories: 345 | Protein: 9.1g | Carbs: 47.8g | Fat: 16.9g | Fiber: 6.7g

Ingredients

- One ripe avocado (halved, pitted)
- One cup of milk
- Half cup of vanilla yogurt
- Eight cubes of ice
- Three tbsps. of honey

Method:

1. Add avocado, vanilla yogurt, and milk in a blender. Blend the ingredients until frothy and smooth.

2. Add honey and ice cubes. Blend the ingredients for making a smooth mixture.

3. Serve immediately.

PART III

Chapter 1: The Fundamentals of a Low Sugar Diet for Diabetics

For people with diabetes, eating can be quite a challenge. After all, it's not easy dealing with the various recommendations made by doctors. The fact is that the following recommended guidelines are essential to keeping your diabetes in check.

You see, it's important to ensure that your blood sugar levels remain in check. One of the easiest and most effective ways to do this is by keeping your sugar and carb intake as low as possible. So, let's take a look at how this occurs when you go on the low-sugar and low-carb, diabetic diet.

Firstly, when you consume carbs and sugars, these are converted into glucose in the bloodstream as the liver metabolizes them. Since carbs are used as a source of energy, the body needs to secrete insulin from the pancreas in order to break down glucose and send it into the cells as functional energy. Then, the body mixes oxygen to create ATP. This is the source of energy that helps you power your body's entire system.

All is good until there is an excess of glucose in the body. When this occurs, the body stores excess glucose as fat. However, there comes a point where the body just can't keep up. This is where insulin resistance happens. In a nutshell, your cells simply stop accepting any more glucose as there is simply too much glucose in the bloodstream.

These are the spikes in blood sugar levels.

This is where the low-carb, low-sugar diet makes a huge difference in your overall health management plan. The rationale is that when you restrict the number of carbs and sugar that you consume, you are basically giving your body the chance to process what's already in the bloodstream and in storage. So, you are creating a deficit that forces the body to use up what it's already stored.

This is how you can get your blood sugar levels in check.

In a manner of speaking, what you are doing is giving your body a break. Therefore, the body has a chance to catch up. When your body eventually catches up, you end up reducing your overall blood sugar levels. In addition, medication is much more effective as there are fewer carbs and glucose to process.

At first, it can be a bit of a psychological shock to think that you have to go on a low-carb, low-sugar diet. In fact, most people think they have to live on lettuce for the rest of their lives. What you will find is that this diet embraces a large number of foods that are very low in carbs and sugar. As a result, you can eat healthy and tasty at the same time.

However, the secret is knowing which foods promote low blood sugar levels. When you discover these foods, you'll find that keeping your diabetes in check doesn't have to be tough. You can still enjoy delicious foods with zero guilt.

Now that's a plan!

Chapter 2: Benefits of a Low Sugar Diet for Diabetics

The low-sugar, low-carb diet is filled with a number of benefits that diabetics can obtain. The best part is that you don't need to wait for an extended period of time to see the benefits. In fact, you can see benefits within a few days of trying out the diet. This is what makes the diet itself so encouraging.

So, here is a list of five benefits you can expect when going on the low-sugar diet.

1. **Reduction in blood sugar levels**

Naturally, this is the most immediate benefit of this diet. As mentioned earlier, when you reduce the amount of carbs and sugar, your body will begin to use up what's already stored in the system. This is why you can begin to see a reduction in your blood sugar levels within a few days. Over time, your blood sugar levels will begin to normalize. So, the diet, along with medication, will prove to be quite effective.

2. Weight loss

Another benefit is weight loss. Since the body converts glucose into fat when it's stored, a reduction in your carb and sugar consumption will force your body to convert stored fat into energy. This is why folks who go on the low-carb diet begin to see weight loss after a few weeks. While this result isn't immediate, it is almost certain that you'll see weight loss, especially if you are overweight.

3. Increased levels of energy

One of the symptoms that accompany diabetes is low levels of energy. This is due to the imbalance that occurs in the metabolism. Since the metabolism cannot keep up with the amount of carbs and sugar in the bloodstream, it does not produce energy as efficiently as it could. As a result, there are lower levels of energy. When you essentially force your body to process stored up fat, your metabolism becomes more efficient in producing energy. The end result is a boost in energy levels. So, don't be surprised if you find at you feel more energetic after a few days.

4. Hormonal regulation

Hormones tend to go out of whack when there are increased levels of blood sugar. For instance, insulin is the first hormone that goes haywire. However, other hormones are affected as well, such as cortisol (it is associated with weight gain) or epinephrine (used to breakdown and release nutrients in the blood). These hormones tend to work inefficiently when there is a high level of blood sugar. As a result, you may not be getting the most nutrition out of the foods you eat.

5. Improved cognitive function

Sugar, in general, works like a fuel in your body. So, when you consume a large amount of sugar, you get the rush that can power you through a given time period. However, sugar is a very poor fuel as your brain burns right through it. The end result is a severe crash afterward. Over time, your brain builds up "gunk." This gunk limits the brain's capabilities. As such, when you replace sugar with other types of fuels, such as vegetable-based carbs, then your brain produces energy more effectively. It's like putting diesel into an unleaded engine. Sure, the car will run, but it will run poorly. This is why many folks on the low-sugar diet report improved cognitive abilities, thereby reducing the phenomenon known as "brain fog."

With these benefits, you can't go wrong with the low-sugar diet!

Chapter 3: Savory Recipe Ideas

Savory Idea #1: Tangy Cabbage Treat

Number of people served: 4

Time you'll need: 33 to 37 minutes

Calories: 253

Fats: 22.8 g

Proteins: 7.9 g

Carbs: 4.7 g

What you'll require:

- Jalapeno Peppers (two, chopped)
- Cabbage (one Head)
- Pepper & salt (as preferred)
- Onion (one, chopped)
- Bacon (six, strips)

What you need to do:

1. Firstly, cook bacon as per the directions on the pack. While you allow the bacon to reach its optimal point, ready cabbage, and onions by chopping into smaller bite-sized morsels.
2. Once the bacon has been prepared to your preference, take it out of the pan and toss the onion and cabbage in. Please ensure to mix up everything with the leftover grease from the bacon while simmering in low fire.
3. Next, get the jalapenos ready by cutting up into pieces as small as you like. Feel free to throw in with the other elements.
4. After the vegetables have reached their optimal point, take the crispy bacon and crumble over the entire mix. Add pepper & salt, along with any other low-carb or low-sugar spices.
5. Lastly, toss everything around until the entire mix is thoroughly even. Serve and enjoy!

Savory Idea #2: Low-carb Egg &Veggie Bites

Number of people served: 6
Time you'll need: 11 to 14 minutes

Calories: 21.8
Fats: 3.7 g

Proteins: 4.3 g

Carbs: 1.8 g

What you'll require:

- Bell Pepper (75 g, Chopped)
- Cucumber (45 g, Chopped)
- Spinach (225 g, Chopped)
- Tomato (75 g, Chopped)
- Eggs (three)
- Salt (as preferred)

What you need to do:

1. To get started, set up oven to 180 degrees Celsius along with a muffin tray. The smaller trays are better as they allow for smaller portions if you wish.
2. Next, use a mixing container and place eggs (cracked) inside. Whisk briskly until they are thoroughly mixed.
3. Now, coat trays with your choice of grease (for instance, non-stick spray). Please ensure to leave some extra for the vegetables (chopped)
4. Then, place eggs in the spaces in the tray and toss in vegetables are per your preference. Please make sure to stir so that the mix is distributed evenly. Then, place in the heat for roughly 11 to 14 minutes.
5. Lastly, make sure to check the mixture is cooked all the way through. Serve as a breakfast treat or yummy snack.

Savory Idea #3: Yummy Chicken Dee-light

Number of people served: 2

Time you'll need: 35 to 40 minutes

Calories: 794.7

Fats: 39.1 g

Proteins: 44.2 g

Carbs: 3.3 g

What you'll require:

- Rosemary Leaves (10 g)
- Pepper & salt (as preferred)
- Garlic (cloves, six, minced)
- Chicken Breast (455 g boneless & skinless)
- Cheddar Cheese (70 g, shredded)
- Butter (55 g)

What you need to do:

1. Firstly, set up your oven to a temperature of approximately 190 degrees Celsius. While the oven gain temperature, prepare a tray with grease (your choice).
2. Next, add seasoning to chicken to your liking.
3. Then, begin to prepare garlic butter. Take pan or skillet and set to medium fire on the range. Once the butter has thoroughly melted, toss in garlic and let cook for roughly five to six minutes. Once this time has passed, garlic should be brownish, but make sure it is not burnt. Now, cover chicken with this butter & garlic mix.
4. Once this mix is prepared, set into the oven for about ½ an hour. Make sure to check the chicken so that it is fully cooked all the way through to the center. Once this has been achieved, add cheese as a topping. Allow to melt.
5. Serve by adding some more butter & garlic mix on top. Enjoy!

Savory Idea #4: Low-carb Fried Chicken Surprise

Number of people served: 6

Time you'll need: 33 minutes

Calories: 768

Fats: 54.1 g

Proteins: 59.2 g

Carbs: 1.9 g

What you'll require:

- Pork (rinds, 85 g)
- Pepper & salt (as preferred)
- Lard (according to need)
- Egg (one)
- Chicken (thighs, six)

What you need to do:

1. First, heat up iron pan or skillet on a range top. Then, place eggs in a mixing container for whisking.
2. Next, prepare rinds by crumbling. Upon completion, coat chicken pieces with egg (you can use a brush or dip) and season as per your liking with salt & pepper.
3. Now, take covered chicken pieces and roll over in the rind crumbs. Do this for every piece.
4. After, add in about half an inch of lard (or cooking oil) into pan or skillet. Wait until it reaches the boiling point. Then, place chicken pieces into the fire. Leave for about four to six minutes on each side. Please make sure they are cooked all the way through.
5. Please ensure to turn chicken around at least twice to ensure proper cooking. Serve with a side of crispy veggies or veggie chips.

Savory Idea #5: Low-Sugar Beef Explosion

Number of people served: 4

Time you'll need: one hour

Calories: 331

Fats: 26.7 g

Proteins: 18.7 g

Carbs: 2.1 g

What you'll require:

- Garlic (cloves, two, chopped)
- Coconut grounds (55 g)
- Onions (green, three)
- Coconut Oil (45 g)
- Ginger (10 g, grated)
- Steak (Flat-iron, 455 g)

What you need to do:

1. First, get steak ready by cutting it up into long, thin slices. Upon completion, place into a large freezer bag so that you can add ginger, coconut grounds, and garlic. Then, place into refrigeration so it can marinate for about one hour's time.
2. Next, put a pan or skillet to heat. Add oil for the meat. Heat up for about three to four minutes until it is at boiling point. Then, toss in steak and let sit until thoroughly cooked. This should take about five to seven minutes.
3. After, add in onions (green) to give the flavor a kick. Let everything sit for a minute or two until the texture is as per your liking.
4. Lastly, take some of the marinade from the freezer bag and add in right before turning off the fire. This will add an extra kick. Serve over zucchini pasta or low-carb couscous.

Savory Idea #6: Tangy Pork Extravaganza

Number of people served: 4

Time you'll need: 34 to 37 minutes

Calories: 466.1

Fats: 32.3 g

Proteins: 47.2 g

Carbs: 2.7 g

What you'll require:

- Stock (chicken, 55 g)

- Pepper (7.5 g)
- Pork (chops, four)
- Milk (202 g)
- Coriander (9 g)
- Thyme (dried, 14.5 g)
- Garlic (cloves, two, minced)
- Butter (47 g)
- Salt (14.5 g)
- Oregano (dried, 14.5 g)

What you need to do:

1. First, get chops ready by placing them on a baking sheet. Sprinkle with pepper & salt to season. Please ensure that seasoning is evenly distributed to guarantee flavor. Let sit for one hour. Once time has passed, carefully rinse chops of excess fluid.
2. Next, set the pan to high heat on range top. Place garlic & butter to stir. Once the garlic is fully transparent, the time has come to add in chops on top.
3. Once chops are placed, cook them through for roughly four to six minutes on both sides. Then, let simmer for another minute, or so, to enable flavors to combine. Remove and set aside.
4. Then, on low fire, throw in stock (chicken), and some milk. Scrape the little leftover bits from the chops. Upon completion, toss oregano, coriander, and thyme in. Please ensure you are only simmering and not boiling the sauce.
5. Lastly, as the sauce thickens, turn the heat off and toss chops back into skillet. Combine all elements and add more pepper & salt if desired. Serve with veggies or a fresh salad.

Savory Idea #7: Filet & Cheese Supreme

Number of people served: 3 or 4

Time you'll need: 31 to 36 minutes

Calories: 211

Fats: 17.4 g

Proteins: 11.9 g

Carbs: 2.25 g

What you'll require:

- Paprika (4.5 g)
- Fish Fillet (225 g)
- Parsley (flakes, 7.5 g)
- Pepper (black, 4.5 g)
- Oil (Olive, 18.5 g)
- Cheese (Parmesan, 45 g)

What you need to do:

1. First, heat up the oven to approximately 180 degrees Celsius.
2. Now, get mixing container for the pepper (black), paprika, cheese (Parmesan), and parsley.
3. Then, cover filets with the spice mix. Add oil (olive) and then rollup the mixture ensuring an even coating.
4. Once the fish is ready, set the filets on to tray and place it into the oven for roughly fourteen to seventeen minutes.
5. Lastly, double-check fish is thoroughly cooked and place cheese on top to create a crust. Let sit for a few moments, until cheese is crispy, remove, and serve. Enjoy with veggies or low-carb brown rice.

Savory Idea #8: Quick and Easy Low-carb Chips

Number of people served: 4

Time you'll need: 28 to 34 minutes

Calories: 91.7

Fats: 8.1 g

Proteins: 3.2 g

Carbs: 2.8 g

What you'll require:

- Salt (as preferred)
- Pepper (as preferred)
- Bacon (slices, eight)
- Oil (Olive, 18.5 g)

What you need to do:

1. First, set up an oven to approximately 180 degrees Celsius.
2. Next, grease a tray with oil (olive) or your choice of grease. Then, break up the bacon into small, bite-sized pieces.
3. After, season with pepper & salt as per your taste.
4. Then, throw into the oven for roughly eighteen to twenty-one minutes. Remove and let cool.
5. Once cool to touch, take bits and put into a skillet, or pan, over medium fire. This process usually takes about four to six minutes. Remove from fire and serve as chips. You can serve with a low-fat, low-carb dip as an appetizer!

Savory Idea #9: Unbelievably Low-carb South Treat

Number of people served: 3 to 4

Time you'll need: 29 to 32 minutes

Calories: 288

Fats: 22.3 g

Proteins: 18.9 g

Carbs: 2.7 g

What you'll require:

- Turkey Breast (roasted, 225 g, chopped)
- Cheese (Parmesan, 75 g)
- Cheddar Cheese (shredded, 225 g)
- White Cheddar Cheese (shredded, 225 g)

What you need to do:

1. First, set up an oven to approximately 180 degrees Celsius.
2. Next, take a mixing container and combine all cheeses. You can whisk or use an electric mixer. Then, take a spoonful of the mix and place onto baking sheet in a clump. Lay down as you would with cookies. Space clumps about one inch apart.
3. Upon filling sheet, throw into over for roughly seven to eight minutes. Please ensure that chips do not get burned. Chips are cooked thoroughly when edges turn light to a golden brown. Then, remove and let cool all the way.
4. Lastly, chop up turkey breast and serve chips with a low-sugar dip. Serve as a snack or entrée.

Savory Idea #10: Low-sugar Italian Snack Option

Number of people served: 4 to 6

Time you'll need: About 22 minutes

Calories: 226

Fats: 23.7 g

Proteins: 18.4 g

Carbs: 5.7 g

What you'll require:

- Mozzarella Cheese (shredded, 225 g)
- Pepper (as preferred)
- Seasoning (Italian, 14.5 g)
- Pepperoni (115 g, chopped)
- Garlic (powder, 8.5 g)
- Salt (as preferred)
- Additional choice: Marinara Sauce for Dipping

What you need to do:

1. First, set up an oven to approximately 180 degrees Celsius.

2. Next, take a small muffin tray and coat with spray (cooking). Leave to one side.

3. Then, in a mixing container, combine pepper & cheese, garlic (powder), salt, and seasoning (Italian). Mix cheese thoroughly and add in the seasoning. Place spoonful of mixture into the bottom of each space on tray.

4. After, top each space with pepperoni. Once ready, place into the oven for about eight to ten minutes. After this time, the cheese should be melted all the way through and light brown around the sides.

5. Lastly, remove, let cool, and serve with low-sugar sauce (marinara works best). Serve as a snack or side for a meat dish.

Chapter 4: Gourmet Recipe Ideas

Gourmet Idea #1: Tasty Chicken and Veggie Pot
Number of people served: 4 to 6
Time you'll need: 26 to 32 minutes

Calories: 238
Fats: 10.9g
Proteins: 27.6g
Carbs: 2.7g

What you'll require:

- Broccoli (one bag, frozen)
- Chicken (115g, shredded)
- Garlic Powder (as preferred)
- Soup (Cream of Mushroom, one can)
- Pepper (as preferred)
- Cheese (Cheddar 221g)

What you need to do:

1. First, prepare the oven to approximately 185 degrees Celsius.
2. Then, in a mixing container, toss in the various elements you will be using (chicken, cheese, and spices)
3. Next, add in soup.
4. Then, place the mixture into a baking container and insert it into the oven.
5. After, let cook in the oven for about twenty-five to thirty minutes.
6. Lastly, ensure that the soup has been thoroughly cooked and cheese properly melted. Serve with a side of crispy veggies or almond breadsticks.

Gourmet Idea #2: Delicious Low-sugar Chicken Meal

Number of people served: 4

Time you'll need: Approximately 30 minutes

Calories: 384

Fats: 21.1g

Proteins: 48.1g

Carbs: 3.2g

What you'll require:

- Cream (Sour, 221 g)
- Salt (9.5 g)
- Chicken (Breast, 1kg, no bone)
- Garlic (Powder, 14.5g)
- Pepper (4.5 g)
- Cheese (Parmesan, 165g, grated)

What you need to do:

1. First, prepare the oven to approximately 185 degrees Celsius.
2. Next, prepare a baking container with grease (or your choice such as spray)
3. After, in a mixing tray, add sour cream and a cup of cheese (Parmesan)
4. Then, place the chicken (breast) into the tray while spreading the mix atop each piece. Also, cover lightly with leftover cheese.
5. After that, insert the tray into the oven. Let it sit there for about twenty-seven to twenty-nine minutes.
6. Lastly, remove once thoroughly cooked and serve with your favorite low-carb side.

Gourmet Idea #3: Italian Chicken Dinner Delight

Number of people served: 2 to 4

Time you'll need: Approximately 25 minutes

Calories: 581

Fats: 41.1g

Proteins: 48.2g

Carbs: 6.1g

What you'll require:

- Garlic (Cloves, two, Minced)
- Tomatoes (Sun-dried, 65g)
- Spinach (221g, Chopped)
- Chicken (Breast, four)
- Paprika (8.5g)
- Cream (Heavy, 221 g)
- Garlic (Powder, 8.5g)
- Butter (14.5 g)
- Salt (8.5g)

What you need to do:

1. First, combine garlic (powder), paprika, and salt into mixing container. Upon completion, use this mixture to coat chicken lightly.
2. Next, fire up a skillet, or pan, and throw in two spoonfuls of butter at the base. Let the butter melt. After this, add in properly seasoned chicken and let cook thoroughly. This would take about five minutes per side. Please ensure chicken is cooked all the way through. Remove and place to one side.
3. Then, add in the rest of the elements: tomatoes, cream, and tomatoes. It will take about three minutes on low fire for the mix to thicken. After, toss in spinach and mix up everything for four more minutes.
4. Lastly, throw the chicken back into the mix so that all flavors can combine. Ensure that chicken is properly cooked and season further if needed. Serve with a side of veggies, zucchini pasta, or low-carb couscous.

Gourmet Idea #4: Yummy Lemon Beef Surprise

Number of people served: 4

Time you'll need: Approximately three hours

Calories: 507

Fats: 35.1g

Proteins: 44.8g

Carbs: 3.1g

What you'll require:

- Pepper (4.5g)
- Lemon (one)
- Garlic (Cloves, four, Crushed)
- Salt (4.5 g)
- Beef (one kg, Cubed)
- Parsley (26g, Minced)

What you need to do:

1. First, prepare the oven to approximately 167 degrees Celsius.

2. Then, prepare a baking container with foil lining.

3. Next, get a mixing container and cover beef (cubed) with juice (lemon), some zest (lemon), salt, and garlic as preferred. Once it is ready to taste, fold over foil to create a small package.

4. Then, when the package is ready, insert into the middle section of the oven and let sit for roughly three hours. This longer cooking time is intended to let the meat soften to its best point.

5. Lastly, remove the package and let sit for about five or six minutes. Cover meat with more juice (lemon) and sprinkle parsley on top. Serve with your favorite low-carb side.

Gourmet Idea #5: Gourmet Sirloin Option

Number of people served: 3 to 4

Time you'll need: 25 to 30 minutes

Calories: 389

Fats: 18.9g

Proteins: 47.1g

Carbs: 2.3g

What you'll require:

- Garlic (Cloves, four, Crushed)
- Oil (Olive, 12g)
- Pepper & salt (as preferred)
- Steak (Sirloin, 945g, Cubed)
- Butter (14.5 g)

What you need to do:

1. First, get an iron skillet or pan and place it on high heat and place oil (olive).
2. Next, add in pepper & salt to the steak as per your preference.
3. Once the steak has been seasoned according to your preference, place it in the hot skillet, or pan, with hot oil. Let the steak in the hot oil for about four minutes on each side. Turnover twice. Then remove. After, using the same skillet, or pan, toss in butter and garlic. Please ensure to move constantly, so the mix doesn't get burnt.
4. When the garlic is light or golden brown. Place meat for another couple of minutes on each side. Let simmer until the flavors are combined. Serve with your favorite side.

Gourmet Idea #6: Unbelievably Low-sugar Surprise

Number of people served: 4 to 6

Time you'll need: Approximately 20 minutes

Calories: 171

Fats: 11.8g

Proteins: 14.6g

Carbs: 2.9g

What you'll require:

- Cheese (Mozzarella, 100g, Shredded)
- Cheese (Parmesan, 75g, Grated)
- Cheddar Cheese (Shredded, 75g)
- Eggs (two)
- Ham (221g, Diced)

What you need to do:

1. First, set up oven to 185 degrees Celsius.
2. Next, get a mixing container so you can combine egg and the various types of cheeses (shredded). After thoroughly mixing, toss in ham (diced) and continue combining until mixture is evenly distributed.
3. After, get a baking container so it can be greased (your choice of grease).
4. Now, separate mixture into eight round balls or rolls.
5. Then, insert the baking container into the oven for approximately twenty minutes. The rolls will be ready once the cheese has melted, and a golden-brown crust has formed.
6. Lastly, remove the dish and allow it to cool. Serve with chicken or any other meat of your choice.

Gourmet Idea #7: Low-carb Salmon Delight

Number of people served: 3 to 4

Time you'll need: 18 to 24 minutes

Calories: 276

Fats: 19.1g

Proteins: 24.5g

Carbs: 3.7g

What you'll require:

- Rosemary (Fresh, two Springs)
- Lemon (55 g)
- Pepper (as preferred)
- Garlic (Cloves, three)
- Salt (4.5 g)
- Salmon (Filets, four)
- Butter (Unsalted, 8.5g)

What you need to do:

1. First, start out by setting the oven to 202 degrees Celsius.
2. Next, line baking container with a sheet of paper (parchment) and set to the side.
3. Then, rinse out filets (salmon) and pat down to try. Upon completion, place on the baking container with the skin facing down.
4. After, take some soft butter to cover the top of the filer. Also, add in some pepper & salt according to your liking.
5. Now, add the spices (rosemary) and the garlic. Cover the filet and insert it into the oven for roughly thirteen to sixteen minutes.
6. Lastly, remove the filet when thoroughly cooked. Add some juice (lemon) to add a tangy zest. Serve with a side of veggies for a nutritious meal.

Gourmet Idea #8: Shrimp-Avocado Treat

Number of people served: 4

Time you'll need: 30 to 35 minutes

Calories: 539

Fats: 45.2g

Proteins: 25.8g

Carbs: 6.1g

What you'll require:

- Onion (62.5g)
- Cooked shrimp (455g, Chopped)
- Eggs (two)
- Seasoning (Seafood, 4.5g)
- Juice (Lemon, 8.5g)
- Parsley (Fresh, 14.5g)
- Crab (Cooked 125g)
- Avocados (four)
- Cheese (Cheddar, 221 g, Shredded)

What you need to do:

1. First, start out by setting the oven to 177 degrees Celsius.
2. Then, in a mixing container, combine the ingredients: eggs, seasoning (seafood), juice (lemon), onion (chopped), cheese (cheddar), parsley, shrimp, and crab.
3. Next, as the stuffing is completed, cut up avocados in half and remove the pit. Then replace the pit with the stuffing.
4. Lastly, insert the avocados in the oven for roughly twenty-seven minutes. Remove from oven and serve with almond breadsticks.

Gourmet Idea #9: Gourmet Hot Pot Surprise

Number of people served: 4 to 6
Time you'll need: Approximately 45 minutes

Calories: 287
Fats: 20.8g
Proteins: 21.9g
Carbs: 4.8g

What you'll require:

- Cheese (Swiss, 70g, Shredded)
- Pepper (as preferred)
- Garlic (Cloves, four, Minced)
- Fish (Filet, your choice, 455g)
- Shrimp (455g)
- Cream (Heavy, 87g)
- Paprika (as preferred)
- Salt (as preferred)

What you need to do:

1. First, start out by setting the oven to 191 degrees Celsius.
2. Next, prepare a baking container with grease (your choice).
3. Then, cut the filet (fish) into small to medium-sized pieces and place them on the bottom of the baking container. Then, place a layer of shrimp on top of the fish. Add pepper & salt as per your liking.
4. After, when you have everything layered, add in garlic and heavy cream to cover. Upon liberally covering, add cheese (Swiss) on top. Add a touch of paprika for that tangy edge.
5. Now, insert into the oven for roughly sixteen to eighteen minutes. Check often to make sure it does not overcook.
6. Lastly, serve with almond bread!

Gourmet Idea #10: Low-carb Tuna Wraps Treat

Number of people served: 4

Time you'll need: About 10 minutes

Calories: 109

Fats: 5.7g

Proteins: 7.8g

Carbs: 7.1g

What you'll require:

- Yogurt (Greek, 50g)
- Wrap (Wheat, four)
- Bell Pepper (Red, 25g, Diced)
- Spinach (45g)
- Celery (65g, Diced)
- Tuna (one can)

What you need to do:

1. First, drain liquid from the can, and place tuna into a mixing container. Once this is in place, add in the red bell pepper, celery, and the Greek yogurt. Combine elements together well, so the vegetables and tuna are combined thoroughly.
2. Next, you are going to want to place the mixture into the middle of the whole-wheat wraps and top off with the spinach.
3. Serve with veggie chips and lemonade for a refreshing brunch treat.

Chapter 5: Quick and Easy Recipe Ideas

Quick and Easy Idea #1: Quick and Easy Veggie Treat

Number of people served: 4

Time you'll need: 35 to 40 minutes

Calories: 51

Fats: 3.1 g

Proteins: 4.5 g

Carbs: 2.3 g

What you'll require:

- Egg (whites, two)
- Spinach (221g, chopped)
- Eggs (whole, two)
- Pepper (Bell, one)
- Salsa (14.5g)
- Onion (35g, chopped)
- Pepper & salt (as preferred)

What you need to do:

1. First, place the pan over medium fire. Once it is warm, throw in some oil (olive) and start by placing spinach and onion until reaching consistency to your preference. Season with pepper plus salt. Add more salsa if you wish.

2. Next, let your vegetables cook, cut up a bell pepper in two slices to create a small bowl. Upon completion, add the spinach mix to the pepper bowls and the open an egg on top.

3. Then, insert into the oven for about 25 to 28 minutes. Make sure to see that egg is thoroughly prepared.

4. Lastly, serve as a side to your favorite meat dish.

Quick and Easy Idea #2: Spicy Egg and Veggie Dash

Number of people served: 12

Time you'll need: 30 to 35 minutes

Calories: 242

Fats: 21.7 g

Proteins: 10.2 g

Carbs: 1.1 g

What you'll require:

- Bacon (in strips, 11)
- Onion (Powder, 4.5g)
- Garlic (Powder, 4.5g)
- Cheese (cream, 95g)
- Pepper & salt (as preferred)
- Eggs (8)
- Peppers (Jalapeno, four, Chopped)
- Cheese (Cheddar, 121 g)

What you need to do:

1. First, fire up the oven to 165 degrees Celsius.
2. Then, fire up bacon until crispy.
3. Next, in another container, mix up chopped jalapenos, eggs, cheese (cream), and seasoning. Toss in leftover bacon grease.

4. Then, take a muffin baking container and fill the edge of each space with bacon. Upon completion, pour in the mix down the middle of each space. Fill up to about 2/3 of the way. This is important as eggs will rise.
5. After, add some cheese (cheddar) and some jalapeno to provide spice. Insert into the oven and let cook for about 22 to 24 minutes. These will be ready when eggs are thoroughly done and fluffy.
6. Lastly, remove and serve as a snack or an appetizer.

Quick and Easy Idea #3: Low-sugar Hot Cake Surprise

Number of people served: 10

Time you'll need: Approximately 20 minutes

Calories: 133
Fats: 11.8 g
Proteins: 5.3 g
Carbs: 1.9 g

What you'll require:

- Flour (Almond, 221 g)
- Eggs (4)
- Milk (Almond, Non-sugar, 36.5g)
- Extract (Vanilla, 7.5g)
- Baking Powder (4.7g)
- Oil (Olive, 18.5g)

What you need to do:

1. First, in a mixing container, mix up baking powder, extract (vanilla), milk (almond), flour (almond), and eggs. Please ensure all clumps are removed.
2. Next, use a tablespoon to place mixture into pan or skillet. Prepare these as you would regular pancakes.
3. Last, top with butter or non-sugar syrup.

Quick and Easy Idea #4: Cheesy Veggie Bites

Number of people served: 4

Time you'll need: Approximately 30 minutes

Calories: 161

Fats: 11.6 g

Proteins: 11.4 g

Carbs: 5.1 g

What you'll require:

- Flour (Almond, 36.5g)
- Onion (36.5g, minced)

- Seasoning (Mexican, 8.5g)
- Mozzarella (221g, shredded)
- Broccoli (225g)
- Salt (as preferred)
- Garlic (clove, one, minced)
- Cilantro (17.5g)
- Egg (one)
- Pepper (as preferred)

What you need to do:

1. First, set up 201 degrees Celsius.
2. Next, prepare a baking container by lining with parchment paper.
3. Then, steam broccoli in a pot (5 minutes) or microwave (1-2 minutes). Tenderize broccoli to make chopping easier.
4. After, cut up broccoli into small chunks. Throw everything into mixing container (parsley, cheese, flour, egg, and spices). Mix up thoroughly until evenly distributed.
5. Now, roll up into a small ball and distribute evenly throughout the baking container.
6. Once completed, cover with some oil (olive) and insert it into the oven for about 26 to 28 minutes.
7. Lastly, serve with low-carb dip as a snack.

Quick and Easy Idea #5: Low-carb Pudding Dee-light

Number of people served: 4

Time you'll need: 18 to 20 minutes

Calories: 132

Fats: 12.1g

Proteins: 13.8g

Carbs: 1.4g

What you'll require:

- Coconut (125g, shredded)
- Almonds (221g, chopped)
- Chia seed (221g)
- Milk (almond, 225g)

What you need to do:

1. First, measure out all of the fixings and add to the Instant Pot, stirring well.
2. Then, secure the lid and select the high setting (2-5 minutes)
3. Lastly, quick release the pressure and place the pudding into four serving glasses.

Quick and Easy Idea #6: Tangy Egg Salad

Number of people served: 4 to 5

Time you'll need: 26 to 32 minutes

Calories: 314

Fats: 25.7g

Proteins: 15.4g

Carbs: 1.4g

What you'll require:

- Bacon (strips, five, raw)
- Paprika (smoked, 14.5)
- Eggs (large, 10)
- Onion (green, 36.5g)
- Mayonnaise (125g)
- Mustard (Dijon, 45g)
- Pepper & salt (as preferred)

Also required: 6-7-inch baking container

What you need to do:
1. First, grease up all sides of the pan inside of pot on the trivet. Toss one cup of cold water in the bottom of the Instant Pot and add the steam rack.
2. Next, open up eggs in a pan.
3. Then, insert pan on rack. Secure the lid and set the timer for 6 minutes (high-pressure). Natural release the pressure to remove pan.
4. After, remove any moisture. Flip pan over on a wooden cutting board for egg loaf to release. Cut up and place it into a mixing dish.
5. Now, clean the Instant Pot container and choose the sauté function (medium fire). Prepare bacon till crispy.
6. After that, add in chopped eggs with mustard, mayo, paprika, pepper, and salt. Top with green onion.
7. Lastly, serve as a side with your favorite meat dish.

Quick and Easy Idea #7: Cheesy Egg Cups

Number of people served: 4

Time you'll need: 12 to 16 minutes

Calories: 117

Fats: 8.8g

Proteins: 8.7g

Carbs: 1.8g

What you'll require:

- Eggs (four)
- Cheese (Cheddar, 125g, shredded)
- Veggies (diced, your choice, veggies tomatoes, mushrooms, and/or peppers, 221g)
- Milk (low-fat, non-sugar, 221g)
- Pepper & salt (as preferred)
- Cilantro (chopped, 125g)

What you'll require for the Topping:

- Cheese (shredded, your choice, 221g)

Also Required:

1. Jars (medium, four)
2. Water (0.5L)

What you need to do:

1. First, whisk up cheese, veggies, pepper, eggs, milk (low-fat), salt, and cilantro.
1. Next, combine the mix into each jar. Tighten lids (not too tight) to keep water from entering the egg mix.
2. Then, arrange the trivet in the Instant Pot and add the water. Arrange the jars on the trivet and set the timer for 5 minutes (high pressure). When done, quick release the pressure, and top with the rest of the cheese (½ cup).
3. Lastly, broil if you like for 2 to 4 minutes till the cheese is browned to your preference.

Quick and Easy Idea #8: Asparagus Appetizer/Side Salad

Number of people served: 4 to 6

Time you'll need: 18 to 22 minutes

Calories: 221

Fats: 8.6g

Proteins: 15.7g

Carbs: 8.1g

What you'll require:

- Red potatoes (small, 455g)
- Asparagus (fresh, trimmed and chopped lengthwise)
- Tuna (2 tins)
- Olives (Greek, 125g, pit removed)
- Dressing (Italian, low sugar, 45g)

What you need to do:

1. First, chop potatoes and let soak in water for about 5 minutes to let starch drain.
2. Next, put water in the pot, about 2 inches, and heat up to a boiling point. Throw in chopped potatoes to cook for about 12 to 14 minutes.
3. Then, in the remaining 2 to 4 minutes of cooking potatoes, add asparagus to the water.
4. After, turn off the heat, remove water from asparagus and potatoes and then place it into ice water.
5. Lastly, serve with tuna and olives as an appetizer or side for a chicken or fish dish.

Quick and Easy Idea #9: Low-carb Pork Treat

Number of people served: 4 to 6

Time you'll need: 18 to 22 minutes

Calories: 221

Fats: 8.6g

Proteins: 15.7g

Carbs: 8.1g

What you'll require:

- Pork (tenderloin, 455g)
- Salt (14.5g)
- Pepper (18.5g)
- Oil (Olive, 75g)
- Cider (apple, 95g)
- Syrup (maple, non-sugar, 25g)
- Vinegar (apple cider)

What you need to do:

1. First, set up your oven to 190 degrees Celsius.
2. Next, cut up tenderloin into two pieces or to fit in the pan or skillet you are using. Transfer into another container.
3. Then, put oil in pan, or skillet, and then fire up for about 6 to 8 minutes. Toss in vinegar, syrup, and cider while adding pepper until boiling point. Make sure to remove bits stuck to the bottom.
4. After, throw in meat. Prepare thoroughly until the mixture is reduced to glazed texture.
5. Lastly, remove and serve while adding sauce for glazing. Serve with a side of veggies.

Quick and Easy Idea #10: Easy Fish Delight

Number of people served: 4 to 6   Time you'll need: 18 to 22 minutes

Calories: 257

Fats: 8.8g

Proteins: 25.7g

Carbs: 9.2g

What you'll require:

- Breadcrumbs (low-carb, 56g)
- Oil (Olive, 45g)
- Dill (fresh, 45g, snipped)
- Salt (10.5g)
- Pepper (5g)
- Filet (tilapia or salmon, 50g per filet)
- Juice (lemon, 25g)
- Lemon (wedges)

What you need to do:

1. First, set up the oven to 186 degrees Celsius. Add the pepper, oil (olive), dill (fresh), salt, and juice (lemon).
2. Next, add filet (fish of your choice) into a baking container which has been previously coated with grease. Add breadcrumbs on top of fish patting down to so they stick. Coat both sides.
3. Then, let sit in the oven until fish is tender, roughly for 12 to 14 minutes.
4. Lastly, serve with veggies and add lemon wedges on top.

Chapter 6: Low-Carb Recipe Ideas

Low-Carb Recipe Idea #1: Balsamic Roast Delight

Number of people served: 4 to 6

Time you'll need: 35 to 40 minutes

Calories: 51

Fats: 3.1 g

Proteins: 4.5 g

Carbs: 2.3 g

What you'll require:

- Chuck roast (one, no bone, 1.5kg)
- Onion (chopped, 55g)
- Water (0.5L)
- Ground pepper (black, 14.5g)
- Garlic (powder, 14.5g)
- Salt (kosher, 14.5g)
- Vinegar (balsamic, 14.5g)
- Xanthan gum (25g)

For Garnishing:

- Fresh parsley (chopped, 20g)

What you need to do:

1. First, combine the garlic powder, salt, and pepper and spread on the meat to prepare the seasoning.
2. Next, utilize the skillet to sear the meat. Add in the vinegar and deglaze the skillet, or pan, while you let cook for another couple of minutes.
3. Then, toss in onion into a pot along with (two cups) boiling water into the mixture. Cover with a top and allow simmer for thirty to forty minutes on medium-low heat.
4. After, remove meat from pot and add to a cutting surface. Shred up into chunks and throw away any fat and/or bones.
5. Now, add in the xanthan gum to the broth and mix up briskly. Place the thoroughly cooked meat back into the pan to heat up.
6. Lastly, serve with a favorite side dish.

Low-Carb Recipe Idea #2: Burger Calzone Treat

Number of people served: 6
Time you'll need: 25 to 30 minutes

Calories: 400
Fats: 25.1g
Proteins: 24.5 g
Carbs: 2.6 g

What you'll require:

- Mayonnaise (45g)
- Onion (yellow, one diced)
- Beef (ground, 750g, lean)
- Cheese (cheddar, 75g, shredded)
- Flour (Almond, 95g)
- Cheese (Mozzarella, 75g, shredded)
- Egg (one)

- Bacon (4 thin strips)
- Dill pickle (4 spears)
- Cheese (cream, 95g)

What you need to do:
1. First, program the oven to 185 degrees Celsius. Set up a baking container with parchment paper.
2. Next, chop up pickles into lengthy spears. Set to one side when completed.
3. Then, to prepare the crust, combine half of the cream cheese and the mozzarella. Insert into microwave 30 seconds. Upon melting, add egg and almond flour to prepare the dough. Set aside.
4. After, set the beef to fire on the stove using a medium temp setting.
5. Now, cook bacon (microwave for approximately four minutes or on the stovetop with pan or skillet). Upon cooling, break up into bits.
6. Now, dice up an onion and toss into the beef to cook until tenderized. Throw in bacon, pickle bits, cheddar cheese, the rest of the cream cheese, and mayonnaise. Move briskly.
7. After that, roll the dough into a prepared baking container. Place the mixture into the middle of the container. Fold up ends and side to create the calzone.
8. Lastly, insert into until brown or about 12 to 14 minutes. Let it rest for 10 minutes before cutting up.

Low-Carb Recipe Idea #3: Steak Skillet Nacho

Number of people served: 3 to 4

Time you'll need: 26 to 33 minutes

Calories: 376

Fats: 31.5g

Proteins: 19.4g

Carbs: 6.1 g

What you'll require:

- Cheese (Cheddar, 75g)

- Coconut oil (45g)
- Butter (15g)
- Beef (Steak, round tip, 1kg)
- Cauliflower (750g)
- Turmeric (15g)
- Chili (powder, 15g)
- Cheese (Monterey Jack, 75g)

For Garnishing:

- Sour cream (25g)
- Jalapeno (canned, 20g, slices)
- Avocado (105g)

What you need to do:

1. First, set up oven temp to 176 degrees Celsius.
2. Next, prepare the cauliflower into chip-like shapes.
3. After, combine the chili powder, turmeric, and coconut oil in a mixing container.
4. Then, throw in cauliflower and add it to a container. Set the timer for 18 to 24 minutes.
5. Now, over a med-high fire in a cast iron pan, place butter. Fire up until both sides are thoroughly done, flipping only one time. Let it sit for six to nine minutes. Slice up thinly and add in some pepper and salt to the meat.
6. After that, move the florets to the pan and add in the steak bits. Top it off with the cheese and bake six to nine more minutes.
7. Lastly, serve with your favorite side of veggies.

Low-Carb Recipe Idea #4: Portobello Burger Meal

Number of people served: 4

Time you'll need: 22 to 27 minutes

Calories: 327

Fats: 23.1g

Proteins:19.4g

Carbs: 6.1 g

What you'll require:

- Mushroom (Portobello, 6 caps)
- Beef (ground, 455g, lean)
- Pepper (Black, 6g, ground)
- Worcestershire sauce (14.5g)
- Salt (pink or kosher, 12g)
- Cheese (cheddar, 56g or 6 slices)
- Oil (avocado, 12g)

What you need to do:
1. First, remove the stem, rinse, and dab dry the mushrooms.
2. Then, combine the salt, pepper, beef, and Worcestershire sauce in a mixing container. Shape into patties.
3. After, fire up the oil (medium fire). Let caps simmer about four to five minutes on each side.
4. Next, move the mushrooms to a bowl, utilizing the same pan, prepare the patties for six minutes, turn, and prepare another six minutes until ready.
5. Now, combine the cheese to the patties and cover for about a minute to melt the cheese.
6. Lastly, add a mushroom cap to burgers along with the desired garnish to serve.

Low-Carb Recipe Idea #5: Low-carb Super Chili

Number of people served: 4
Time you'll need: 20 to 24 minutes

Calories: 319
Fats: 24.1g
Proteins:39.2g
Carbs: 3.4g

What you'll require for the Chili:
- Stock (beef or chicken, 25g)
- Steak (1kg, cubed into 1-inch cubes)
- Leeks (sliced, 25g)
- Cumin (4g)
- Cayenne pepper (ground, 4g)
- Pepper (black, 4g)
- Salt (4g)
- Whole tomatoes (canned with juices, 221g)
- Chili powder (2.5g)

Additional Toppings:
- Cheese (cheddar, 221g, shredded)
- Sour cream (95g)
- Cilantro (fresh, 25g, chopped)
- Avocado (one half, sliced or cubed)

What you need to do:
1. First, toss all of the fixings into the cooker - except the toppings.
2. Then, use the cooker's high setting for about six hours.
3. Lastly, serve and add the toppings.

Low-Carb Recipe Idea #6: "You won't believe it's low-carb" Chicken Parmesan

Number of people served: 2 to 4

Time you'll need: 34 to 40 minutes

Calories: 586

Fats: 31.4g

Proteins: 55.5g

Carbs: 2.7g

What you'll require:

- Rinds (pork, 221g)
- Sauce (Marinara, 45g)
- Chicken (breast, 455g)
- Cheese (parmesan, 56g)
- Garlic (powder, 12g)
- Pepper & salt (as preferred)
- Egg (one)
- Cheese (Mozzarella, 125g, shredded)
- Oregano (12g)

What you need to do:

1. First, set up an oven temp setting of 165 degrees Celsius.
2. Next, utilize a food processor to mash rinds and cheese (parmesan). Add them to a mixing container.
3. After, pound chicken breasts until they are about one-half inch thick. Whisk up egg and dip chicken in for the egg wash. Place the chicken into crumbs.
4. Then, distribute the breasts on a lightly greased baking container evenly. Add in seasonings and insert them into the oven for approximately 23 to 26 minutes.
5. Now, cover with the marinara sauce over each serving. Top with the mozzarella and bake for 12 to 14 minutes.
6. Lastly, serve with a bed of spinach.

Low-Carb Recipe Idea #7: Tangy Coconut Chicken

Number of people served: 4 to 5
Time you'll need: 25 to 28 minutes

Calories: 492
Fats: 39.7g
Proteins:28.9g
Carbs: 2.3g

What you'll require for the Tenders:

- Egg (large, one)
- Onion (powder, 8.5g)
- Curry (powder, 18.5g)
- Pork rinds (Crumbled, 125g)
- Chicken (thighs, 1kg, no bone or skin, about 6 to 8 pieces)
- Coriander (14.5g)
- Coconut (shredded, 95g, unsweetened)
- Garlic (powder, 8.5g)
- Pepper & salt (as preferred)

What you'll require for spicy and sweet mango sauce dip:

- Sour cream (25g)
- Ginger (ground, 14.5g)
- Mango extract (15g)
- Mayonnaise (25g)
- Sugar-free ketchup (25g)
- Cayenne pepper (14g)
- Liquid stevia (7 to 8 drops)
- Garlic (powder, 8.5g)
- Red pepper (flakes, 5g)

What you need to do:

1. First, program oven to 185 degrees Celsius.
2. Then, whisk the eggs and debone the thighs. Slice them into strips (skins on).
3. Next, add the spices, coconut, and pork rinds to a zipper-type bag. Add the chicken, shake, and place on a wire rack. Bake for about 14 minutes. Flip them over and continue baking for another 18 minutes.
4. Lastly, combine the sauce components and stir well. Serve with your favorite side of veggies or salad.

Low-Carb Recipe Idea #8: Slow cook Chicken Casserole

Number of people served: 3 to 4

Time you'll need: 35 to 45 minutes

Calories: 224

Fats: 9.4g

Proteins:30.4g

Carbs: 5.7g

What you'll require:

- Chicken breasts (two in cubes)
- Bay leaf (one)
- Cheese (Mozzarella, 221g, shredded)
- Tomato sauce (256g or one tine)
- Seasoning (Italian, 14.5g)
- Salt (5.5g)
- Pepper (4g)
- Optional: slow cooker (2-quart)

What you need to do:

1. First, remove the bones from the chicken and chop it into cubes. Add them to the slow cooker.
2. Next, pour in the sauce over the chicken and add the spices. Stir and cook on the low setting for thirty to forty minutes.
3. Lastly, serve with the cheese as a topping.

Low-Carb Recipe Idea #9: Low-carb Roll Up Treat

Number of people served: 2 to 4

Time you'll need: 15 to 20 minutes

Calories: 191

Fats: 7.9g

Proteins:15.6g

Carbs: 1.9g

What you'll require:

- Eggs (large, 6)
- Milk (221g)
- Garlic (powder, 14.5g)
- Salt (kosher, 9.5g)
- Pepper (Black, 9.5g, freshly ground)
- Butter (11g)
- Chives (chopped, 5g)
- Bacon (slices, 12)
- Cheese (cheddar, 105g)

What you need to do:

- First, in mixing container, whisk up eggs together along with milk and garlic (powder). Add in salt & pepper as preferred.
- Next, in skillet or pan, melt butter over medium fire. Toss in eggs and scramble for 2 to 4 minutes. Toss in chives.

- Then, on a cutting surface, cut up bacon slices. Place cheddar on the bottom and then toss in a bunch of eggs. Roll up very closely.
- Lastly, place rolls back into pan, or skillet with the seam facing down. Remove once crispy. Serve with whole-grain toast.

Low-Carb Recipe Idea #10: Cauliflower Cheese Surprise

Number of people served: 2 to 4

Time you'll need: 10 to 20 minutes

Calories: 164

Fats: 6.5g

Proteins: 16.3g

Carbs: 2.4g

What you'll require:

- Cauliflower (one Head, about 256g)
- Eggs (two)
- Cheese (parmesan, 75g)
- Oregano (35g)
- Cheese (cheddar, 75g, shredded)

What you need to do:

- First, cut up cauliflower into individual florets. Place them into a food processor until the texture appears similar to rice. You could also grate if you don't have a processor.
- Then, in a mixing container, combine cauliflower, eggs, cheese (parmesan), and the oregano. Mix up until even and add salt & pepper.
- After, fire up a skillet, or pan, over medium fire. Todd mixture into the pan. Pat down to form a patty. Exert pressure using a spatula. Cook for 4 to 6 minutes. Turn over and repeat on the other side.
- Lastly, sprinkle cheese until it is melted. Make "sandwiches" by putting two pieces together. Serve as a snack or side to your favorite meat dish.

Chapter 7: 7-day Sample Low Sugar Diet Plan

In this chapter, we are presenting a 7-day sample plan to give you an idea of how you can put together a winning combination of healthy foods. Please bear in mind that this is only a guide. So, feel free to customize this plan as you get more experience and develop your own style.

	Week One		
Day / Meal	Breakfast	Lunch	Dinner
Monday	Fresh fruit bowl topped with granola and honey	Veggie and chicken club sandwich on whole wheat bread	Chicken and veggie casserole
Tuesday	Spicy breakfast burritos	Bean soup with croutons	Grilled salmon and veggies
Wednesday	Scrambled eggs, bacon and a slice of whole-grain toast	Mixed garden salad, fresh veggies, and grilled chicken	Sirloin and veggies surprise
Thursday	Low-sugar cereal with low-fat	Steak and potatoes with a	Chicken fajitas with mashed

	dairy milk	side of crispy veggies	potatoes
Friday	Veggie cheesy bits	Grilled salmon, sautéed veggies with garlic whole wheat toast	Roast beef club sandwich with crispy plantain bits
Saturday	Low-sugar whole grain flapjacks	Spicy chicken fajita burritos	Veggie pizza with small salad
Sunday	Whole grain veggie breakfast wraps	Tangy Mexican bean bowl with guacamole	Chicken noodles and sautéed veggies

Printed in the USA
CPSIA information can be obtained
at www.ICGtesting.com
LVHW020942191223
766860LV00005B/287